PRAISE FOR DREA

M000035180

"Like a grove of aspen trees that appear to stand independently yet their roots are connected, Patti Fields' dreams speak to me as though I am the dreamer. Her gentle guidance removes the lens from my ego and places it over my heart. There are no prerequisites for this book. Be open, be brave, and listen to what God has to say to you."

REV. MARY RAMERMAN
Former pastor, Spiritus Christi Church

✦

"Patti Fields' dreams and visions are modern day parables like Jesus shared in the Bible. The wisdom is still relevant today. *Dreaming Miracles* helps our modern mind remember Truth, God, and Love. They are packed with the potential to transform."

SEEMA KHANEJA, MD
Author of *Physician Heal Thyself – A Doctor's Journey from Medicine to Miracles*
www.coachingforinnerpeace.com

✦

"When Patti Fields shares her dreams and visions, I listen carefully because of the deep wisdom they convey. *Dreaming Miracles* will help you uncover hidden blocks and hidden treasures. The Spirit is always speaking to us. I invite you to open the pages of this book and listen."

REV. BARBARA ADAMS, M.S.ED.
Author of *The Adventures of the Course Kids: Through Faith and Grace*
www.peaceandharmonyministry.org

"The singular mind of Consciousness communicates with us through symbols that often appear in our dreams. The dreams and visions Patti Fields shares in *Dreaming Miracles* help us to access the deep wisdom within and offer insights for us all. They become OUR dreams, OUR wisdom, and OUR healing."

SABRA DEFOREST
Shamanic Practitioner

◆

"The opportunity to see truth can come to us in many ways. The messages shared in *Dreaming Miracles* are my opportunity to recognize and heal the blocks in my own life that I didn't know existed."

EMILY L., MSW

◆

"The dream messages shared in *Dreaming Miracles* are inspirational, interesting, and engaging. They have helped me uncover unconscious patterns and discover spiritual insights. I now know that I too can receive answers and change my thinking."

RUTH C., LCSW

DREAMING MIRACLES

How One Person's Dreams and Visions Benefit You

DREAMING MIRACLES

Spiritual Messages That
Help and Heal

✦ DREAM PRACTICE GUIDE INCLUDED ✦

PATTI FIELDS

ARS METAPHYSICA

an imprint of Sunbury Press, Inc.
Mechanicsburg, PA USA

ARS METAPHYSICA

an imprint of Sunbury Press, Inc.
Mechanicsburg, PA USA

For information about special discounts for bulk purchases, please contact Sunbury Press Orders Dept. at (855) 338-8359 or orders@sunburypress.com.

To request one of our authors for speaking engagements or book signings, please contact Sunbury Press Publicity Dept. at publicity@sunburypress.com.

FIRST ARS METAPHYSICA EDITION: May 2021

Set in Adobe Garamond | Interior design by Crystal Devine | Cover by Lawrence Knorr | Edited by Abigail Henson.

Publisher's Cataloging-in-Publication Data
Names: Fields, Patti, author.
Title: Dreaming miracles : spiritual messages that help and heal / Patti Fields.
Description: First trade paperback edition. | Mechanicsburg, PA : Ars Metaphysica, 2021.
Summary: *Dreaming Miracles* interweaves the author's intimate experiences of universal hardship, profound answers from the spiritual realm, inspiring examples of healing, and practical tools for transformation to help YOU experience miracles—complete freedom from unconscious beliefs and patterns, trauma, and pain.
Identifiers: ISBN : 978-1-62006-489-4 (softcover).
Subjects: BODY, MIND & SPIRIT / Healing / Prayer & Spiritual | BODY, MIND & SPIRIT / Dreams | SELF-HELP / Spiritual.

Product of the United States of America
0 1 1 2 3 5 8 13 21 34 55

Continue the Enlightenment!

You will first dream of peace, and then awaken to it.

—A COURSE IN MIRACLES

Dedicated to my daughters,
Chelsea, Amanda, Alyssa, and Jessica—
my angels on earth and in spirit.

Contents

When we are willing to ask questions
and search for true understanding,
we become open
to the healing power of the spiritual realm.
That is why,
whenever I am in need of answers,
I close my eyes with faith
that the Spirit will speak to me.
I wake up grateful
for the amazing insights and healing I received.

—PATTI FIELDS

I.

How it all Began

How hard is it to stand on the edge of a cliff
and simply let yourself fall?
How much energy does that actually take?
You see? You let yourself fall.
You abandon yourself to the absence of control
and you fall into the underlying everlasting
arms of Love—of God.

—THE RAJ MATERIALS

THE NIGHT I buried my baby, Amanda, I experienced my first spiritual dream:

As I enter the catacomb, the darkness envelops me. I have no idea where I am going. All I know is that I need to keep moving. I step slowly toward what I think is a rock and blindly feel along its edges with my hands while being careful not to trip or fall. The climb becomes steeper and the rocks jagged with not much more than six inches of a surface on which to place my feet. Below is a fiery pit of hot flames and bubbling lava. If I make one wrong move, it will all be over. Frightened and alone, I forge ahead. Each step robs me of strength and weakens my resolve.

The path of darkness and struggle seems endless. I hear my hopeless thought echo off the rocks, "I don't think I can survive." As I near the top of the mountainous terrain, I place my foot on a rock. It wobbles. I start to sway. I don't have the strength to steady myself. I give in and fall over the cliff. As the flames reach up to meet me, I declare to myself, "It all ends here." Suddenly, an enormous hand comes down from the heavens and swoops me up just before the flames touch me. In the blink of an eye, everything changes. No longer falling to my death, a strong, protecting hand cradles me. No longer frightened and alone, I rest safely in God's loving embrace.

When I awoke the next morning, I shared the dream with my mother. Her eyes began to fill with tears. She whispered with a mix of reverence and gratefulness, "God spoke to you." At that moment, I realized something extraordinary had happened.

The experience of being cradled in God's protection and love kept me from going over the edge. It gave me the strength and courage to navigate this new terrain called "grief." It was my reminder during the dark days ahead that I didn't need to hold myself up. I could surrender and fall into the loving arms of God.

When I received the message that God was carrying me safely through this experience, I knew nothing about spiritual dreams. Like many of you, I dreamed of being chased by scary monsters, showing up naked at work, and forgetting my locker combination. But, after Amanda died, all that I believed up until that moment made no sense. The religious rules I was living by failed me. With everything falling apart, something cracked open. And, there it was—a channel to spiritual wisdom I didn't know existed.

Since my first spiritual dream, I have received many won-drous communications from the spiritual realm. These Divine messages come during times of great distress or confusion. They offer guidance and incredible insight. I find them helpful, gentle, and sometimes funny. And, most importantly, they provide a source of healing and blessings for me and others.

II.

Dreams and Visions:
A Connection to Guidance
and Wisdom

Putting yourself to sleep awakens you to
spiritual consciousness.

—FROM THE TEACHINGS OF EDGAR CAYCE

WHEN I began seeking answers to life's most difficult questions, it didn't take long to realize the intellect's limitations. I wanted answers that made sense—answers that provided true understanding and healing.

Previously, I had understood that dreams were a fascinating tool that connected me to the unconscious mind. After my first spiritual dream, I realized that dreams could connect me to a deeper level within the unconscious mind that contains spiritual wisdom. Through these types of dreams, I gained spiritual understandings that no amount of intellectual study could provide. With the messages I received, I soared to new heights of spiritual awareness and broke free from years of limiting beliefs and unhealthy patterns that might have otherwise taken weeks, months, or even years to accomplish.

Receiving spiritual messages and using dreams to connect to the spiritual realm is nothing new. History books and spiritual writings recount several occurrences when mystics, visionaries, prophets, and even ordinary people received profound messages outside normal consciousness. We all can connect to this level and receive spiritual messages. It's just a question of how deep within our minds we're willing to go.

Think of the mind as a house with many floors. The first floor contains our daily mental activity—all conscious thoughts during our waking life. This cognitive thinking helps us function at work, complete tasks, have coherent conversations, and fulfill our primary responsibilities. From the first floor, we go down the basement steps where our beliefs, memories, judgments, and thought patterns are stored—generally referred to as the ego. Many of our dreams originate from this unconscious level, but it is not the lowest level in the house. From the basement, we can access a secret passageway that leads down to another level where our spiritual insights are stored.

Even though this level is available to us all day and all night, we usually stay on the first floor, seldom going down into the basement and rarely, if ever, entering the secret passageway. What keeps us from reaching this deeper level of our mind? While awake, thoughts about our daily living and earthly problems, past experiences, and future worries are all-consuming and monopolize our attention. Unable to quiet our minds, it is difficult to access the spiritual level.

Another challenge preventing us from reaching this deeper level is our belief that spiritual guidance could require sacrifice or be painful to hear. Rather than quieting our minds and listening to the Spirit, we spend time analyzing our problems and trying to solve them independently.

We might also be afraid to discover unpleasant unconscious thoughts and feelings that lurk in the basement. Deciding that it is safer to repress and deny them, we do not let our awareness travel below the first floor.

Although it is possible to overcome these obstacles through sheer will and determination, I find it easier to bypass them by simply going to sleep.

When we sleep, we retire from the external world with all its problems and concerns and naturally relax our thinking and defenses. This process enables us to connect with the unconscious mind effortlessly. By combining this practice with our desire to listen to spiritual wisdom, our dreams become a way to obtain wisdom and guidance from the spiritual level.

NOT ALL DREAMS ARE SPIRITUAL MESSAGES

Some dreams can be scrambled messes. They result from the unconscious mind creating an imaginary world of symbols that interact in a chaotic and nonsensical way. Most of these dreams contain thoughts and beliefs from the superficial level of the unconscious. I generally don't pay much attention to these dreams. They originate from just below the first floor without much wisdom or clarity to be helpful.

Other types of dreams bring repressed feelings and judgments to the surface, making us conscious of them. For example, if our boss reprimands us at work, we might become angry and upset. Afterward, we might dream that we are on stage, and everyone is laughing at us. This dream is helping us get in touch with our feelings of shame and inadequacy. This realization is a good thing. Awareness is the first step in the healing process, and dreams can facilitate this.

However, this book is about a different kind of dream—dreams that awaken us to the truth of who we are.

SPIRITUAL DREAMS

Spiritual dreams are God's way of speaking to us and our opportunities to listen. They provide new and sometimes surprising insights that cannot be gained through intellectual study or the ego. In addition to helping you notice a pattern or clarify your understanding of a problem, a spiritual dream can help you change how you look at things and guide you to take action. Spiritual dreams can also provide information about future or past events, your life's purpose, and what is most beneficial for your soul's growth.

This kind of dream helped me get in touch with the presence of Divine love and brought me miracles—complete freedom from years of old beliefs, patterns, trauma, and pain.

VISIONS

In addition to dreams, spiritual visions offer powerful insights. They occur while you are awake or in a meditative state.

Visions awaken you to a new state of mind. They expand consciousness—lifting you out of the earthly realm and into the spiritual realm. During a vision, one feels a profound sense of peace and love. Visions can include but are not limited to: images, light, sounds, feelings, or a deep intuitive sense of spiritual reality.

Regardless of whether we experience a spiritual dream or a vision, both are passageways that lead us to profound wisdom and healing.

III.

Universal Messages That Help and Heal You

What is most personal is most universal.

—CARL R. ROGERS

YOU MIGHT be wondering how it is that my dreams and visions can help YOU. I wondered the same thing. For years, I did not share my dreams or visions with others. I considered them to be personal messages about my blocks, fears, and confusions. Then, when I began teaching *A Course in Miracles (ACIM)*, I shared the messages to make a point or illustrate an answer to a question. The students' reactions surprised me. Many expressed how my messages clarified confusing principles, revealed their unconscious patterns, provided answers to their deepest questions, released fear, or helped them connect to their inner Spirit. A friend summed it up in this way: "I feel that your dreams and visions are modern-day parables similar to those Jesus shared in the Bible. The wisdom is still relevant today. Your dreams help us remember Truth, God, and Love."

This understanding and use of dreams is nothing new. In Western society, we tend to view dreams as "playing out" individual problems and concerns. We believe the messages received only benefit the dreamer. But, in some cultures and religions, dreams are viewed quite differently. For example, in certain indigenous communities, a visionary or Shaman will travel into the dream world to seek clarity, healing, and guidance for the whole community. In early Christianity, dreaming was a highly regarded way to receive messages from God. The Bible includes several stories about ordinary men and women, prophets, and kings who received dream messages and shared them to benefit all.

What do these cultures and spiritual communities know that modern societies may be slow to recognize? They know we are all connected through a collective unconscious. What appears to be a personal problem can be universal. What seems to be a solution for one can be helpful to all. The evidence of these truths is all around us.

Have you ever shared an experience with someone, believing it was yours alone, only to learn that they also had the same experience? You may recall instances when you've had an identical thought as someone else or immediately after thinking of another person, they call you on the phone or physically appear.

In addition to these, I've experienced the same dream, on the same night, as another person. I've also received and written in my journal an insight that was identical to my friend's journal writing that same morning. Once, I received a dream message specifically for a woman I knew but hadn't spoken to in weeks. I did not know that she had prayed for help with a challenging issue before going to sleep. During my dream that night, I received a hopeful picture of what was to come into her life. When I shared it with her the following day, she exclaimed that the dream was an answer to her prayers. Soon after receiving this dream message, a surprising new opportunity came her way.

These are all examples of how we are all connected by an invisible bond and can influence one another in profound and positive ways. The most compelling evidence of our connectedness for me is when the dream and vision messages I receive help and heal others.

IV.

How to Use This Book
for Healing

A dream that is not understood remains a mere occurrence;
understood it becomes a living experience.

—CARL JUNG

SPIRITUAL DREAMS and visions have a purpose. They are a way for the Spirit to guide us toward wholeness by revealing new understandings and healing unconscious false beliefs and self-destructive coping patterns. Through entertaining short stories and creative symbolism, we can learn how to avoid mistakes, overcome obstacles, and change the direction of our lives.

However, to fulfill this purpose, we need to integrate what was received unconsciously with our everyday life's conscious level—our relationships, work situations, struggles, grievances, and any source of dis-ease. To facilitate this process, each chapter in this book begins with a quote related to the message received. After the description of the dream (or vision), I provide insights to help clarify the message. Contemplation questions are included after each commentary to aid in personal exploration. These questions will help you reflect on the message as if the Spirit is speaking directly to YOU. This process will enable you to experience breakthroughs in areas that seem the most blocked.

There can be an even more significant benefit of spiritual dreams and visions which is easy to overlook. Sometimes the dream or the vision itself can be the healing. In other words, just by having the experience (without contemplating, interpreting, or applying the message), you become free of the block, fear, or pattern that previously existed. I've encountered this experience in my life when upon waking, the healing had already occurred. I've also noticed this change in others, sensing a shift as they hear the message. For you, this means reading the dream or the vision as if it were your own. Imagine that YOU have asked for the Spirit's help, and this is the answer to YOUR request.

GOD HAS MANY NAMES

Research indicates that there are more than 900 names and titles for "God." With so many options, how can we choose? Can a name possibly encompass all that this Supreme Being is? And what if a name upsets someone? Should we avoid using it? I frequently thought about this quandary when writing about spiritual matters in this book.

After careful consideration, I chose to use a few different names (Spirit, God, Presence, The Divine, and Creator) to identify the source of these messages.

If you notice a resistance or adverse reaction to one of these names, most likely, it is because the word conjures up a negative characteristic such as angry, condemning, punishing, or authoritative. Or perhaps, the word is affiliated with a specific religious doctrine you don't support. If this happens, you might choose to ignore the message or "close the book." Unfortunately, this response closes your mind to teachings that can be helpful.

Although it is important to disconnect from negative associations, it is equally important to remain open-minded. To accomplish both, you can think of a name as a symbol—a word representing something. Then, focus on the qualities the name represents. As an example, if you were to read the word "apple," you would immediately move past the word and begin to formulate in your mind a red, rounded fruit that tastes sweet or tart.

You can use this same process when reading one of the many names for the Supreme Being. Move past the word to the qualities the name represents (all-loving, all-knowing, all-good, eternal, changeless, holy, gentle, or patient). Another option is to substitute a name that you believe better represents the Supreme Being's true nature.

The method used does not matter. The most important thing is to find a way to quiet any resistance. By doing so, you remain open and ready to receive the blessings and healing contained within these messages.

My hope is that the spiritual messages in this book will remind you of the Spirit's presence in your life. As my dreams and visions become yours, may you be healed and blessed in infinite ways.

Let the dreaming begin. . . .

DREAMS

Follow your dreams. They know the way.

—Kobi Yamada

V.

Let Love Guide You, Not Fear

Be very still and open your mind. Go past all the raucous
shrieks that obscure your eternal link with God. Sink deep
into the peace that waits for you beyond the frantic, riotous
thoughts and sights and sounds of this insane world.
We are trying to reach the place where you are truly welcome.
We are trying to reach God.

—A COURSE IN MIRACLES

BACKGROUND

Sometimes, situations and circumstances in life are so scary that we become anxious and panic even after years of spiritual practice. When fearful, it seems impossible to turn away from the problem, quiet the mind, and listen to spiritual guidance. For me, this occurred during a major change in my life. After years of being a stay-at-home mom, my divorce was final, and I needed a way to support myself. All my energy and attention went into résumé writing and searching for a job. Deep down, I knew fears were driving my actions, and it would be better to meditate and receive guidance, but I couldn't sit still. All the things I relied on for safety and security were gone! I had to DO something. Each time I would try to sit and meditate, the ego response sounded like this: "Do nothing? Are you crazy? You can't just sit still. You don't have time!"

I continued to frantically search for what I should do next until one night, in total frustration, I asked, "How can I trust that going within will actually solve my problems?" Little did I know that when I closed my eyes and fell asleep, the answer I received would be a miracle.

DREAM

I am standing on the Titanic right at the moment when we discover the ship is sinking. Everyone, including me, is trying to figure out a way to survive. Panic ensues as hundreds of people rush to get to the upper deck, scrambling over one another to grab life jackets and find lifeboats. Some passengers take their chances and jump into the frigid water, hoping a boat will eventually come to their rescue. I stand paralyzed in fear. How can I make a choice when none of these options seem to be a sure bet? Suddenly, I notice a beautiful, loving Presence standing in front of me.

This Presence is pure light, calm, and peaceful—a stark difference to the rest of us on the boat. It speaks to me. "Come and follow me. I know the way that will save you." I immediately feel a sense of relief; someone knows the way! I lean in closer to hear what choice I should make. The Presence continues, "Here's what we must do. We must go to the very bottom of the boat." There is a split-second pause, as I wonder, did He say bottom?

"What!" I scream out loud, "The bottom? But that's insanity and sure death. How can that be the way?" Apparently, the Presence doesn't know the laws of physics and never saw the ending to the movie "Titanic."

And yet, the Presence remains certain and calm. He points to all the frantic people going up while explaining, "What they don't

18

know is that the act of hitting the very bottom of the boat creates a propelling motion that raises you out of the boat and onto dry land with no effort at all on your part."

I try to see the logic here, even though my mind silently argues with the insanity of going in the opposite direction of everyone else. But then, I sense the Presence's confidence and consider going to the bottom.

At this moment, however, I decide that I would feel a lot better about my choice if others would come along with me, so I ask, "Why isn't anyone else following us down to the bottom?"

The Presence calmly responds, "Because they can't hear me."

I take a quick look around and see that this is true. Everyone is screaming in terror and can't hear the Presence speak about this other way.

Even though I still think going to the bottom is crazy, I take comfort in realizing that the Presence is 100% certain. I take His hand, and we enter an elevator. As the doors close, my heart beats faster. Doubt creeps in. This solution seems insane, but there is no going back now. As we descend to the bottom of the boat, the water level rises to meet my feet—terror strikes as I watch the small ripples lap over my shoes. I look to see how the Presence is reacting to our impending doom. Even the rising water does not sway His calm and certainty. I am reassured, yet still confused about how we will survive.

The water reaches waist high and continues to rise. I begin to wonder what it will be like when the water covers me completely and I can no longer breathe. As I imagine our inevitable fate, an invisible force pushes the water away from me and toward the elevator door. It's like the parting of the Red Sea! The water is not engulfing me. I can breathe. I stare in disbelief at the wall of water in front of me. How can this be? This makes no sense. It's impossible! And then it dawns on me. The Presence must not operate under this world's laws, and when I took His hand, I placed myself under new laws—ones where miracles happen. My last thought before I woke up was, "From now on, things are going to be different!"

COMMENTARY

Many of us are running for our lives in one way or another—scrambling to grab onto something or someone to keep us safe. We attempt to control situations, cling to another person, stay excessively busy, or gather material possessions, believing these are the lifeboats to keep us afloat. We engage in these behaviors without being fully aware of the fear that motivates them. Why? Well, it would just be too frightening! Before this dream, I knew I was acting out of fear. Yet, I was unaware of how terrified I was until I found myself standing on the Titanic at the moment the ship was sinking!

When onboard a sinking ship and believing you need to do something to survive, dropping deep down within the mind to connect with Divine love and peace seems insane—until you realize that going in this direction leads to miracles.

Receiving this nighttime assurance, I awoke the next morning with less fear and more faith. I calmly put aside my résumé and search for a 9-to-5 job and started a daily meditation and listening practice. Whenever the ego screamed, "Do something!" I remembered that the ego's solutions provided no guarantees. I drew strength from the Presence's certainty that the answers exist within us. When I noticed sabotaging thoughts such as *I won't have enough money to survive* or *no one will take care of me*, I let them go. And then, I chose to remember that Divine solutions are always loving, helpful, and miraculous. Each time I decided to respond to fearful thoughts in this way, the ego's voice faded away while the Presence's messages grew more frequent and profound.

Things began to fall into place.

Opportunities to facilitate study groups and host retreats materialized. Creative ideas for new programs began to flow. Newfound strength and wisdom gave me the power to get things done and with a successful impact. Following the Presence's lead, I became a spiritual mentor, author, and teacher—a radically different career direction than what I had expected.

This dream is a powerful reminder to all of us that even during our most terrifying moments, we are never without help. It's true that the ego shrieks the loudest when the "ship is sinking." But, if we pause long enough to question the ego's solutions and quiet our minds, we will hear a gentle voice speak of another way. So, the next time you are acting out of fear and grabbing on to what will NOT save you, remember the miracle in the elevator, and trust in the direction the Presence is leading you. You may be concerned or even doubtful about the sanity of this direction. That's OK. Just keep going. But, consider yourself warned: as you let the Presence lead you deep into the mind, miracles WILL happen.

CONTEMPLATION

Be You in charge. For I would follow You,
certain that Your direction gives me peace.

—A COURSE IN MIRACLES

+ Think of a problem that you need a solution to—one that causes anxiety and fear.

+ List all the possible solutions that require you to do something.

✦ Review each solution and notice any concerns or doubts that it will work. (Doubting the ego's solutions is the first step to trusting the Presence.)

✦ As you consider these solutions, say to yourself, "Even though I think I need to do these things to be 'safe,' I will lay them aside so I can learn another way."

✦ Acknowledge the Presence by focusing your mind on this: "I am not alone. The Presence is here with me and will guide me to a solution that will work."

✦ Using your own words, set an intention to go within and listen to the Presence's answer.

✦ If you become fearful, pause and remember that the Presence wants you to be happy and safe and would never lead you into danger.

✦ Let any insights, feelings, senses, and guidance arise in your awareness. Notice how the Presence leads you to new opportunities, answers, and healing in the days ahead. If you become fearful, call on the Presence and ask for help, and it will be given to you.

VI.

Remove the Blocks
to Abundance

*I love to see the beings being set free from the hypnosis of
conditioning: from fears, false projection and the grip of ego.
And I know that to be liberated is not difficult, in fact it is
natural. However, it requires great openness and the
sincere and earnest desire to be free.*

—Mooji

BACKGROUND

This dream occurred during a time when I was feeling
frustrated and discouraged. I wanted a fulfilling career,
financial stability, and to feel safe and loved. But, no matter how
many affirmations I repeated, I continued to feel uncared for
and unloved. I finally made a sincere appeal to the Spirit, asking
for awareness of what was blocking good from coming into my
life. The answer was shocking. I had no idea THIS existed in
my unconscious mind! Yet, the Spirit's response was just what I
needed. Once I acknowledged and let go of the blocks, I began
to experience abundant blessings and gifts in my life.

I am standing in a dimly lit room. There is just enough light to see a small four-foot-high pedestal table. As I solemnly approach the table and stand before it, I notice a mound of brown clay.

With great reverence and care, I begin working with the clay. I first mold a body and then shape a bit of the clay to make a blanket. I lay the body gently and tenderly on top of the blanket. Noticing some bright red clay, I take it and form the letter "J" and then place it at the clay figure's feet.

From the shadows, a kind and gentle voice asks, "Why are you putting the letter "J" there?"

I passionately reply, "Because everyone deserves to be remembered by their name, no matter what they have done!" I then construct a noose out of the remaining clay. I carefully place it around the body's neck to show he had committed a terrible crime and was hanged.

Filled with compassion, I place a statue of Jesus beside the lifeless form. I strategically position it, so Jesus is looking down while one hand is on his heart, and the other hand is extended outward toward the clay body. This statue's placement gives me some comfort.

Suddenly, a loud voice breaks the somber silence. Startled, I turn around to see a gray-bearded man wearing a gold-encrusted vestment robe and a jeweled crown emerging from a dark corner in the back of the room. His face and ears are fiery red, and he is fuming with anger. He rushes toward me, wags his finger, and bellows, "Get that statue away from him. He does not deserve to be anywhere near Jesus!"

His abrupt and harsh command frightens me to tears, and I step back. But, when I realize he wants to take the Jesus statue away, I become indignant. Someone must defend this person's right to be loved, even if he is a sinner! I stand tall, face him, and cry out,

"Jesus loves everybody! Jesus loves everybody! Jesus loves everybody!"
I wake up with these words on my lips and tears streaming down
my face.

COMMENTARY

I once heard a story about a man who was trying to manifest his soul mate by repeating the affirmation, "My perfect soul
mate is with me now." He placed written notes of the affirmation
around his apartment, car, and office. One day a colleague points
to one of the notes and asks, "How is that working for you?"
The man replies, "Not very well. I knew no one would want to
be with me." After the dream, I realized I had a lot in common
with the man in this story. I had no idea that while I passionately
proclaimed my right to be loved and cared for, I unconsciously
believed I wasn't good enough and didn't deserve it.

This dream reveals a startling realization. Deep within our
unconscious mind is a belief that we are "bad" and unworthy;
and this is the reason we are not experiencing abundance in all
areas of our lives. This makes sense when we understand that our
beliefs have a powerful effect on our life experiences. *A Course in
Miracles* teaches that "every thought you have either brings peace
or war; either love or fear" (W.pI.16.3:1). Imagine then, what
a thought of unworthiness would bring! When we experience
punishment or deprivation, it is not because God demands it;
rather, it's because we unconsciously believe we deserve it.

With this new awareness of what was blocking abundance, I
reviewed situations in my life to determine if I did believe this.

+ When needing help from others, I was hesitant to ask
  because I felt unworthy of their time and energy.

- ✦ While trying to grow my business, I was fearful that the programs I offered would be unsuccessful, and I would lose money because I thought I was incompetent and not good enough.

- ✦ When I didn't receive an invitation to a social engagement, I felt excluded and assumed I had done something wrong.

In each of these situations, I experienced or expected punishment and deprivation. The evidence was clear—I must have an unconscious belief in unworthiness.

I then thought of all the futile ways we try to get what we want even though deep down, we believe we are unworthy. We demand that others appreciate and support us. We loudly declare our right to be loved. We make an effort to obtain love by "doing the right thing," pleasing others, or sacrificing. Or maybe, as the dream indicates, we try to feel some comfort by believing that Jesus still loves us, despite our sin. Why don't these attempts result in feeling cared for and FULLY loved? Because there remains a subliminal voice screaming from a dark corner within our minds, "You don't deserve love!" And we believe it.

As I pondered this dilemma of our desire for more, while believing we are undeserving, I had a flash of insight. It's not that God loves us despite our sin. He loves us because we are holy and, therefore, deserving of blessings. And, if God does not condemn us to a life of misery, then why would we continue to listen to a voice that does?

I wiped away the tears and wrote in my journal, "The days of self-condemnation are over." From that day forward, whenever I noticed a desire to experience abundance in an area of my life, I honored it. If I had a negative expectation or a thought that I was undeserving, I did not try to cover it up with an affirmation. I acknowledged the block and asked the Spirit to show me that I am innocent and deserving because I am a child of God.

Over the next few months, I noticed a change. An overall feeling of well-being replaced my frustration. I didn't hesitate to ask friends for help, and they were willing to assist. The programs I offered were well attended and rewarding. I received invites from friends who seemed eager to include me in their gatherings.

Although discovering what beliefs lurk in the dark corner of my mind was uncomfortable, learning that I deserved God's abundant blessings felt wonderful! So, if you feel uncared for or unloved, take comfort in this dream's message. What you believe about yourself is not true. You ARE worthy and deserving.

CONTEMPLATION

Those who discover the reality of their inmost being enjoy lasting peace, love and wisdom. These are the fruits of authentic self discovery.

—MOOJI

+ To get in touch with your deepest desires, sit quietly and reflect on this question: What would you like to feel or experience? For example, you might want to experience financial security, a loving relationship, a sense of purpose, or you might want to feel appreciated, peaceful, or safe. Avoid thinking about how it should appear and focus on the experience you want to have.

+ Allow time to feel the longing for the experience while reminding yourself that this is what God wants for you, too.

✦ Review each desire and notice any sabotaging thoughts or beliefs of unworthiness or guilt. To heal these thoughts or beliefs, recall a time in your life when you felt unworthy or guilty. As you relive this situation, let any emotions and physical sensations arise. Do not judge yourself, your beliefs, or your feelings. Instead, be thankful for your willingness to acknowledge them.

✦ These beliefs have stayed with you and are the blocks preventing you from receiving what you desire. It's now time to let them go. With faith and trust, ask the Spirit to provide new experiences that will teach you that these beliefs are not true and that you are deserving of God's abundant blessings.

✦ Become aware of the many gifts God is making available to you. For instance, you may notice an opportunity of interest presenting itself, a friendly gesture of support, a new relationship unfolding, a positive change occurring without struggle or effort, or an overall sense of well-being. These gifts are offered to show you that you are innocent and deserving of God's blessings.

✦ Remember, the key to living an abundant life is to know that you are deserving of it. Give thanks to the Spirit each time you learn this beautiful lesson.

VII.

Break Free from Limitations

There is no need for help to enter Heaven for you have never left. But there is a need for help beyond yourself for you are circumscribed by false beliefs.

—A COURSE IN MIRACLES

This spiritual message was given to me during a time in my life when I was feeling stagnant, unfulfilled, and bored. I wanted to live a fulfilling life, yet my attempts to expand into new opportunities, develop new relationships, and get out and enjoy life were unsuccessful. I couldn't figure out what was holding me back.

Have you ever felt this way? Have you ever wondered why things don't change even though you desire something more? The following dream reveals a startling answer that has the power to radically change your life like it did mine.

DREAM

A plane lands on a tropical island. I depart the plane with the other passengers. As we place our feet on the soft, plush grass, we marvel at our surroundings. *Rolling hills and rainbow flowers, sounds of ocean waves, and singing birds welcome us to paradise. Feelings of peace and joy wash over me. My heart beats with excitement, and I am eager to explore the island. As we stroll along, taking in the sights and sounds, I hear whispers. At first, just one or two whispers, but then more people join in, "Wolves. This place has wolves." I look around in disbelief. Paradise can't have wolves! But then I see one near the bush, and then another one behind the tree. My mind begins to register the danger we are in; a silent scream catches in my throat. At this moment, chaos erupts. Everyone runs in different directions, scrambling to find something that will protect them from the wolves.*

Out of nowhere, enormous cages appear. Each cage consists of a thin frame and flimsy mesh walls. The door is merely a screen draped over the frame with a simple latch that is easy to open. Despite their fragile appearance, we all run to the cages and quickly close the door.

In my cage, we huddle together, trembling. We see a wolf approach the cage. A wave of murmurs spreads through the group. "Will it attack? Will it get in? Are we going to die?" But, they do not attack. They do not show their teeth. They just sniff around. Eventually, they wander in between the other cages and then disappear over the horizon. We begin to relax. The wolves are out there. We are in here. We are safe. We settle in and occupy ourselves with mundane activities. We read, eat, engage in small talk, and sleep. Days and weeks pass. We find a rhythm and a resignation to living inside the cage.

One day, someone notices a tear in the mesh—familiar panic ripples through the group. "Quick, fix the mesh!" a man screams. A group of us hurry to secure the opening. On another day, the door latch becomes loose. Alarmed, others fumble to latch the door.

After many days without a wolf sighting, our small talk turns to questions. "Are the wolves still out there? Is it safe to leave the cage?"

As if listening for their cue, wolves appear in the distance, reminding us just to be content with what we have.

Several days later, while I am standing at the edge of the cage looking through the mesh at the rolling hills, beautiful flowers, and crystal-clear water, I see something for the first time. Outside the cage, there are people. People are playing tennis, swimming in the water, and picnicking on the grass. People are laughing and carefree. People are not afraid. How had I not noticed people outside before? Had they always been there, and I just hadn't seen them? Waves of shock turn to wonder. If the people outside the cages are safe and happy, then perhaps the wolves have gone. Or, there are wolves, but the wolves aren't dangerous.

With these new thoughts and wonderings came questions I had never thought to ask, "Can I be free and happy, too? Can I live outside this cage?"

COMMENTARY

According to the Gospel of Thomas, the disciples approached Jesus and wanted to know when the kingdom of heaven would arrive. Jesus explained that the kingdom of heaven is here now, yet men do not see it (G. Thom. 113).

This dream conveys the same message. Heaven is not just an internal spiritual experience. The entire world is heaven. God's love and beauty are everywhere. Opportunities to connect with others and share in the joys of life are here now. This dream beckons us to open our eyes and look beyond our small world of routine and limitation (our "cages") and see all the gifts God has made available to us. It's not a matter of where to go or what we need to do to earn these gifts. It is a matter of letting go of the fear and false beliefs that keep us from stepping outside our "cages" and receiving them.

I learned from this dream that buried beneath my willingness and earnest prayers to have an expansive, joy-filled life lay one of my deepest fears. I was afraid to follow my passions, be open to new opportunities, and develop new relationships because I believed that I would be harmed or suffer in some way. Many people have a similar fear. As a result, we build our walls and choose the security of our "cages" to protect us. Content with our routines, rules, and limitations, we believe it's much safer to live this way. And, it is THIS misguided belief that keeps us from our most profound treasures.

In the dream, when I noticed people living safely in paradise, I had an astounding realization. For years, I had lived in a "cage" because of this unconscious belief that wasn't even true! I could feel the shift in my thinking immediately upon waking. In the days and weeks that followed, I noticed a change. No longer afraid to expand my horizons, I explored new career opportunities and learned new skills. I ventured out, met new people, engaged in new activities, and had more fun. Finally, a deep and limiting belief had been transformed. As a result, the fear of expansion had vanished.

Imagine what a precious gift it is to others if we are willing to follow our heart's desires, "step outside the cage," and allow this Divine energy to guide us. When others see how carefree, joyful, and safe we are, the spell of fear is broken. For this reason, when you feel the stirrings of desire for new opportunities, relationships, or adventures, pay attention. You are beginning to open your eyes and see the beauty that surrounds you. You are remembering that God never intended for you to "live in a cage."

If you realized that living a vibrant, expansive, creative life is not dangerous and is helpful to others, what choice would you make? Would you "step outside the cage?"

CONTEMPLATION

I will not be afraid of love today.

—A COURSE IN MIRACLES

+ In what area(s) of your life do you feel like you are trapped or "living in a cage?"

+ Write down adjectives or phrases that describe your current situation.

+ Ponder this question: What beliefs and fears keep me from living an expansive, abundant life? Write down whatever comes to mind.

+ Place a question mark after each belief and fear to indicate your willingness to learn that the belief might be false and the fear unwarranted.

+ Now, write down what you would like to experience in these areas of your life.

+ As you review the list of desired experiences, repeat slowly out loud or silently, "God intended for me to have a joyful, purposeful, and inspiring life. It is safe to be open to God's love and care."

+ Relax and be aware of any feelings, insights, or guidance you receive.

+ As you go about your day, become aware of new inspirations, opportunities, and relationships that present themselves.

+ As you take action steps, you may become fearful. To help strengthen your faith that there is nothing to fear, call to mind people you know who live life in this way, who live outside the cage of limitation, and are peaceful and happy.

+ Remind yourself as you "step outside the cage" that it is safe to receive God's gifts and live a joy-filled life.

VIII.

Dissolve the Barriers
Between Us

*You have no idea of the tremendous release and deep
peace that comes from meeting yourself and your
brothers totally without judgment.*

—A Course in Miracles

During my early years as a spiritual teacher, it was cost-
effective to host study groups and classes in my home.
I advertised online, in newspapers, and by word of mouth. As
a result, many new people began attending these events. This
increased interest was both exciting and nerve-racking. I enjoyed
meeting new people and exploring different points of view;
however, I was concerned about opening my home to strangers.
Fearful that someone might have malicious intent, I decided I
would close the events to new members. Although I did not
want to exclude others from our community, this was the best
way to protect myself and my daughters. It never occurred to me
to ask for spiritual guidance. When decisions had to be made
regarding the safety of my children, I thought I knew best.

I peacefully fell asleep, relieved that I had found a solution. However, the Spirit had a different view, and it was shown to me in my dream that night.

Are you sometimes wary of strangers or people who seem different than you? Do you keep your distance from those who do not share your values and beliefs? Do you limit your circle of friends because you feel uncomfortable when meeting new people? Do you isolate yourself from others because you are afraid of being hurt? The barriers that we place between ourselves and others may seem to keep us safe, but they also prevent us from connecting with others and experiencing love. How then, can we connect intimately with others, love everyone, and at the same time, feel safe? This dream message shows us the way.

DREAM

I sit inside the screened porch of the cottage that I share with friends, resting after a hard day's work. I look out over the moonlit water that surrounds our island home. There is no sign of land for hundreds of miles, yet being isolated from the rest of the world does not disturb us. Our group is small, but we co-exist amicably.

The cottage is active this time of night. As friends prepare the food for our evening meal, my thoughts and eyes wander. When I spot the shadowy figure standing on the dock peering out at the water, my heart skips a beat. Even though this man shares our island, he is a stranger to us. We haven't met him, nor do we want to. We can tell by how he lurks around the dock that he is mean and has malicious intent. We try to enjoy our daily existence, but we can never fully relax while living under the constant threat of being harmed.

Tonight, while preparing dinner, we keep a watchful eye on his movements. He sits and bows his head. He glances up at the house—we freeze. He looks back at the water—we relax. Fearing we might do something to agitate him, we move cautiously and speak in hushed voices. While friends bring food to the table, I stand inside the screen porch and monitor his movements. I can't believe what I'm seeing. . . . Is he approaching the cottage? What could he want? Did we do something to upset him? I must warn the others. A strained whisper escapes my lips. "He is coming!"

Panic strikes. Instantly, everyone abandons the dishes and food and gathers near me. We huddle together for safety. By now, he is standing outside the screen door. His face, cast in diamond shape shadows, looks ominous. "What will he do to us?" a friend asks in a quivering voice. No one replies because no one knows. He has never approached the cottage before. Poised to defend ourselves, we wait for his next move.

"I'm hungry. Can I have some food?" Baffled by his question, no one responds. "This must be a trick to get inside the house," I announce under my breath. "Maybe we should give him what he wants," a friend suggests. "Opening the door is dangerous," another friend warns, "but we don't want to provoke him." A few indecisive seconds pass, then reluctantly, everyone nods their agreement to give him what he wants.

Friends frantically prepare a plate of food and pass it quickly to me. Fumbling with the latch, I carefully open the screen door and slip him the plate of food. We hold our breath waiting for his next move. He turns and walks away. We exhale a collective sigh of relief, but our fear remains. What if he comes back?

Just then, a thunderous noise turns our attention toward the open waters to the left of the cottage. "Is that a speedboat?" I wonder in astonishment. When I realize that the boat is heading right toward us, I cry out to the others, "If the driver lands here, he will be trapped on the island with this man, too." Desperate to save the driver from our fate, we swing our arms wildly and repeatedly shout, "Go away! You don't want to come here!" The driver ignores our warnings. We stare in dismay as the boat comes closer and closer to the cottage. Twenty yards, ten yards, ten feet, five feet . . . the boat touches the shoreline, skids across the grass, breaks through the screen, and finally comes to a full stop inside the porch. We are stunned and confused.

The driver, eagerly jumping out of the boat, flashes us a bright smile. He is a large man with rosy cheeks, a long white beard, and a round belly. There is something wise and endearing about him. Without pause, he cheerfully greets everyone with an enthusiastic handshake. "Hello. I'm pleased to meet you. How are you?" We all start talking at once. "You have to leave. It's not safe here. There is a dangerous man who lives on the dock. Leave while you can!" The driver responds with a smile and continues to shake everyone's hand. I whisper to my friend, "The man from the dock doesn't know he is here. There is still time to convince the driver to leave." Then, I spot the shadowy figure standing outside the screen door. My heart sinks. It's too late. Now the driver will be imprisoned too.

Before we can warn the driver to keep away from the door, the unthinkable happens. The driver, noticing the man, rushes to the screen door and swings it wide open. We cower, expecting the worst. To our amazement, the driver draws the man to him, envelops him in a big bear hug, and exclaims with unbridled joy, "I'm so happy to see you!" We stare at each other in disbelief. How could he hug him!

When the driver releases the man and steps aside, we see him clearly for the first time. What we see is unbelievable. The man's presence is loving and peaceful. His mannerisms are graceful. His eyes sparkle with kindness and warmth. We look at each other, shocked. How could our judgments have been so wrong? How could we ever have been afraid of such a caring and gentle soul?

COMMENTARY

I awoke the following morning feeling grateful for the Spirit's intervention and the startling message I received. Having learned that my perceptions of others might not be accurate and that my fears could be unfounded, I am free from worry—until the phone rings a few hours later.

A man calls and asks for information about the study group that I am hosting in my home that evening. He explains that he learned about the meeting from an online advertisement and is interested in attending. A feeling of dread washes over me. I know where this conversation is headed. Finally, he asks the inevitable question, "What is your home address?"

My thoughts race. *What if he is dangerous? What if he finds out that I am a single mom with three daughters and then returns when no one else is around?* Before I can inform him that the group is closed to new members, it dawns on me—this situation is similar to last night's dream! This realization turns my thoughts and questions in a new direction. *Maybe my judgments are inaccurate. Perhaps he is not dangerous. If I could see him through the eyes of the Spirit, what would I see? How would I feel? What would I do?* Then I ask the question that puts all other thoughts and questions to rest: *Why not apply what I learned from the dream to this situation and see what happens?* Trusting that coincidences are winks from the Divine, I give the man my home address.

At seven o'clock, the doorbell rings. Feeling anxious, I reluctantly open the door and invite the man into my home. We quickly move through the pleasantries. As I take his coat and hang it in the closet, he says shyly, "You look familiar." I turn around to face him and realize he looks familiar to me, too. Dusting off old memories, I search for our connection. Then, we both remember at the same moment—he was the director of the homeless shelter where I volunteered twenty-five years ago.

This man had a significant impact on me as a young adult. I admired how he treated everyone with dignity and respect, offered support and guidance without judgment, and responded lovingly to everyone regardless of economic, physical, or behavioral differences. As I share these thoughts with him while standing in the foyer, a tender moment passes between us. We enjoy our "small world story," and then he walks into the family room and takes a seat in the circle. I pause before following him. With a silent chuckle, I raise my eyes to the heavens and whisper, "Now THAT is a great way to help me learn to trust Your teachings."

When we are willing to let go of our judgments and solutions and trust in the Spirit's teachings, we can perceive everything through a spiritual lens. And, THIS is how we release fear, and foster love and connection.

When I was a young spiritual student, I would retreat to remote places for a few days of silence and contemplation. In the dark of night, I would challenge myself to walk in the woods without a flashlight. The purpose of this practice was to learn how to control my fear. Inevitably, everything took on a nightmarish quality. Upon "seeing" ghosts, ferocious animals, and strangers hiding in the bushes, I would succumb to fear and frantically run back to the cottage. One evening, I decided to take a flashlight with me. When something frightened me, I would point the light toward the object. Surprise! The ghost was a tree rustling in the wind. The ferocious animal was a tiny, harmless squirrel. The stranger ready to attack behind the bush was a deer munching on his dinner. It was amazing how different things appeared in the light!

Instead of looking at others through the ego's dark lens and becoming frightened, we can let the Spirit shed light on what we see. When we perceive others through a spiritual lens, our feelings will naturally shift from fear to love. How can we apply this practice to the people who cross our path? The following story is a great example.

A woman once told me about a problem she was having at her workplace. Her boss's constant criticism and unrealistic expectations made her work life intolerable. One morning while driving to work, she ruminated over her boss's misconduct. Angry, she decided that she needed to confront her boss. She began mentally constructing a list of wrongdoings and demands that she would cite when she arrived at work. Suddenly, a voice interrupted her mental reprimands. The Voice said with an air of authority, "She is My child too."

Hearing these words, the woman perceived her boss in a new way, and her anger disappeared. However, she didn't realize the magnitude of her change of heart until she was face to face with her boss. Instead of seeing someone who deserved punishment, she saw a fatigued and worried person who deserved kindness and support. The woman, overcome with love and concern for her boss, spontaneously asked, "How can I help you?" With a look of relief, the boss explained the pressure she was under and how much the woman's offer meant to her. Together they came up with a plan to meet their work goals. They remained friendly and continued to work well together.

When we see a reprimanding boss, an attacking driver, a self-serving politician, an unloving family member, an uncaring friend, or a suspicious stranger, we may be tempted to attack, judge, and exclude them. Separating ourselves from others will never provide the love and connection that we need to heal our world. Recognizing the Divine essence within every one of us, however, will.

Misperceptions produce fear and true perceptions foster love.

—A COURSE IN MIRACLES

When we perceive someone negatively or are afraid of them, it is tempting to put up barriers to protect ourselves. This contemplation exercise can help dissolve the barriers between us by allowing the Spirit to guide our perceptions of others.

+ For this exercise, select someone you fear, dislike, or disagree with because they do not share your values or ideas. You'll know the one to choose when you consider whom you want to exclude from your life.

+ Notice your judgments and feelings when you think of this person. Make a mental note of your desire to exclude or separate from them to feel safe.

+ Ask yourself, "Do I want to experience judgment and separation or love and connection?" Before answering, remind yourself that:

  + You can experience love and connection without being in physical proximity to someone. This reminder will help you answer the question honestly.

  + You do not need to convince yourself that your judgments are wrong. You need to decide which is more valuable to you—the dark cloud of judgment or the light of their divinity. If you choose judgment, you are choosing fear and separation. If you choose divinity, you are choosing love and connection.

+ Now, make your decision. Rest assured that if you decide to hold on to your judgments, their divinity will always be there for you to see whenever you are ready.

+ After you decide to experience love and connection, the awareness of their divinity will come to you in many ways. Trust that whatever you receive from the Spirit is in the best interest of everyone. Remain open. Notice how you feel, what you see, and what thoughts come to mind about this person. Listen for any inspired action.

+ In your own way, express gratitude for this new way to feel love, connection, and safety.

IX.

Heal the Hurt

Our subconscious minds have no sense of humor,
play no jokes, and cannot tell the difference between reality
and an imagined thought or image.

—ROBERT COLLIER

BACKGROUND

One evening during a conversation with a friend, I became agitated. Her criticism, disregard for my opinions, and disdain for my choices rattled me. Feeling hurt, I made-up an excuse to leave. When I returned home, I thought about our conversation. How could she treat me that way? How could I continue to be friends with someone who doesn't care about my feelings or my perspective? Feeling justified, I considered ending our friendship.

Before falling asleep, I tearfully prayed for relief from the hurt caused by her words. To my surprise, instead of having a dream that offered me consolation and sympathy, I was given a lesson in cause and effect. Unmistakably, I learned that when I decide what something means, it not only determines my feelings and perceptions, it prevents me from seeing the truth. Until

I was willing to question my interpretation of the conversation, peace would continue to elude me.

Are you hurting because of what someone said or did? Are you wrestling with emotional hurts from the past? This dream message teaches that any upsetting situation can be resolved if we are willing to question our interpretations and allow spiritual wisdom to prevail.

DREAM

I apprehensively approach the front door of the house. An acquaintance from work has invited me to join her and her room-mates for dinner. Uneasy about having a meal with strangers, I knock timidly. The door swings open. A man's smiling face and cheerful welcome put me at ease. "Hello. Come on in. We've been expecting you." Entering the living room with a bit more enthusiasm, I take a seat on the couch. As I listen to the lively music and good-natured bantering, I sit back and let myself relax, thinking this evening will be enjoyable.

Beeeep! "What was that noise?" I cry out in alarm. My question lingers in the air. The friendly chatter continues. No one else seems to be concerned. I wring my hands nervously, as my eyes scan the room for an explanation.

Noticing my distress, a man explains, "No worries. The noise means that the electrical system is turning on." Sure enough, the room spontaneously floods with the glow of lamplight and the sounds of a television program. A moment later, the television screen changes to black without any warning and the room darkens. Confused, I turn to the man to help me understand what this change means.

"No worries," he says with a grin, "The electrical system turns on, but then within seconds, it turns off again."

"How strange," I mutter under my breath. But, I accept his explanation without question.

Content, I decide to explore the rest of the house. I wander through the living room toward the kitchen. Hovering at the entryway, I notice the kitchen is buzzing with activity. A few people stand at the range, stirring and tasting the food cooking in pots. Others mill around the center table, arranging silverware and plates. My eyes rest on a young couple peeling and slicing vegetables at the sink. Their heads bend toward one another, creating an intimate cocoon amidst the bustle of activity. While admiring their loving energy, I hear the woman say, "Oh, my ring!" Laughing, her hand reaches into the garbage disposal.

Beeeep! Oh no! The man's explanation skips across my mind . . . a warning . . . electrical system . . . off . . . on. . . . Rigid with fear and unable to scream or run, sickening waves of dread wash over me. I shut my eyes. I can't bear to see what comes next. But, I feel, hear, and see every disturbing detail: the metallic rattling of clogged, grinding gears, shrilling screams, mangled fingers, excruciating pain, and squirting blood. In anguish, I pray for the painful sights and sounds to stop.

Just then, I feel the energy of a loving presence behind me and hear a calm and gentle voice ask, "How do you know what is happening? You have your eyes closed." Shockingly, I remember now. The sights and sounds seemed so real that I forgot I had closed my eyes. "Oh my gosh," I remark in astonishment. "I could be imagining the whole thing!"

COMMENTARY

Waking from this dream, my viewpoint of the situation with my friend completely shifted. Although I was asking for the

Spirit's help, I hadn't realized that I had been unwilling to let go of "my story." Therefore, the first step to heal the hurt was for me to acknowledge that my perspective could be wrong. Reflecting on the conversation with my friend, I recognized a pivotal moment when I closed my mind to what was happening and began filling in the moment with my own meaning. My interpretation was indeed heartrending. And, based on my feelings and perceptions, it seemed accurate. But, listening to the Spirit's question in the dream gave me a reason to pause and reconsider. Could my interpretation be wrong?

With this question, my mind opens. I am now ready to listen. I ask the Spirit, "What do I need to understand about the conversation with my friend?" Instantly, I have an overwhelming sense of my friend's admiration and love for me. My heart expands with feelings of love for her. The tears flow, but this time they are tears of relief.

A few days later, while having coffee with my friend, I share my experience of our previous conversation and the dream I had. She laughs good-naturedly and says, "That's not what I was saying at all. I said just the opposite. I was expressing how much I value your opinion and how much I have learned from you. Wow, you do have a wild imagination!"

It can be easy to forget that our interpretations influence how we feel and what we perceive in times of upset. It can be difficult to remember that what we think we see happening or what we think we are hearing may not be accurate. These ideas seem impossible to fathom when what we perceive and feel is so upsetting! Yet, this is a major point of the dream message. Our interpretations can create intense feelings and experiences, but that doesn't mean they are true.

Consider how many ways there are to interpret an event. Imagine that someone has an appointment with you and they are late. This event can be experienced in a multitude of ways. If you interpret lateness as rude, you will feel angry. If you decide that their late arrival gives you unexpected free time, you will feel grateful. If you interpret their tardiness as selfish, you will feel unappreciated. With so many different interpretations, how can you know the meaning behind their action?

Consider how often people's experiences can differ even though everyone is witnessing the same event. Each person can have a completely different interpretation of what happened and be equally convinced their version is the "truth." That is because our thoughts and feelings offer strong evidence that we are right. But, what if our senses are reporting faulty information?

Years ago, I participated in a sacred spiritual ceremony that took place in a small tent. While sitting in the cramped, dark space, there was a moment when I literally couldn't breathe. Petrified that I was going to lose consciousness, I proclaimed, "There isn't enough oxygen in here! I have to leave!" When the leader opened the flap of the tent, a stream of light illuminated the circle. I quickly glanced at the other participants and noticed that they were all breathing normally. When I realized that my mind was playing tricks on me, I could suddenly breathe without strain—proof that even our physical sensations can be misleading.

Learning to question our interpretations during times of distress is a valuable skill. Yet, how can questioning our inter-pretation lead to healing the hurt? An analogy of filling a mug with coffee can help us understand the link between letting go of our story and healing. Imagine that you are holding an empty mug. You look inside and see the word "peace" written at the bottom. If that same mug is filled with coffee, the word "peace" is no longer visible. Likewise, if you fill a worldly event with your interpretation, you cannot experience peace or feel joy. It is only after you "empty out" or remove your meaning that you can hear the Spirit's message. And, the Spirit's message always leads to peace.

For years, my former husband would fall asleep on the couch in the late evening even after I requested that we use this time to connect. To me, sleeping on the couch meant that he didn't care about my needs, did not want to spend time with me, and didn't love me. Once, while walking past the couch and feeling the familiar hurt, a thought crossed my mind. *Maybe this doesn't mean what I think it does.* With this opening, a spontaneous question emerged. "Spirit, what does it mean?" The Spirit's answer came in the form of a vision.

Suddenly transported back to my childhood home, I am a little girl looking at my dad, who is fast asleep on the couch. I tap him on the shoulder. "Daddy, daddy, daddy." No response. My eyes fill with tears as I think to myself, *He doesn't love me. He doesn't want to spend time with me. He doesn't care about my needs. I am all alone.* Then something unique happens. I can feel my dad's emotions and hear his thoughts. I feel his stress and worry. I feel his physical exhaustion. I hear his thoughts of concern about business matters and how he will provide for his family. And then, I feel how deeply he loves me. In a flash, I return to the present moment. I glance at the couch. The hurt is completely gone, and all I feel is love.

A friend criticizing me and a father or partner ignoring me are upsetting images. And, so is a hand in a garbage disposal! Maybe you have a few distressing images of your own. Do you perceive someone rejecting you, mistreating you, or telling you that you don't matter? Stop for a moment and consider that what you hear, see, or feel is based on your interpretation, and your interpretation IS painful. The Spirit's interpretation, however, is loving and will lead to peace. Which one will you choose?

CONTEMPLATION

If your intuition says, "It's time to let go of a personal story,"
the mind may project a doubt and fear of losing something of
value. But if you really feel this inside your heart,
Grace will take you beyond needless suffering
into your natural being.

—MOOJI

If we want to heal the hurt, we must be willing to question and let go of our interpretations because only an open mind can learn the truth. The following exercise can help.

+ Think of a situation when you felt betrayed, unappreciated, or hurt in some way.

+ Do not judge yourself. It takes courage to be honest about how you feel. Allow yourself to feel your emotions while at the same time acknowledge that your interpretations may be affecting how you feel.

+ Next, it's important to separate your feelings from your interpretations, so you do not get bogged down with emotion. Freely write or say out loud what you think their actions, words, and gestures mean. Resist the temptation to judge yourself or others while you explore your interpretations. Focus on your inner thoughts rather than what might be motivating others. Keep in mind that without Divine guidance, you cannot know what's going on.

✦ Use the "test of truth" to decide if you want to cling to your interpretations. Ask yourself:

  ✦ When I interpret the event in this way:

    ❖ Am I free of fear?

    ❖ Am I at peace?

    ❖ Do I feel love for myself and others?

  ✦ If the answers are "no," then consider that your interpretations may be wrong.

✦ In your own words, express willingness to release your interpretations. If emotions are so strong that it is difficult to let go of your meaning, you can use this phrase to encourage release:

  ✦ "Even though I feel _____(unloved, angry, scared), I am willing to let go of my interpretations and listen to spiritual wisdom because I want to feel love, peace, safety, and joy."

✦ Be still and listen.

✦ Express gratitude for any insights, feelings, and perceptions you receive.

VISIONS

A Voice will answer every question you ask, and a vision will correct the perception of everything you see.

—A Course in Miracles

X.

Replacing Fear with Love

We are all Vibrational Beings.
You're like a receiving mechanism.
When you set your tuner to the station,
you're going to hear what's playing.

—ABRAHAM-HICKS

When we are gripped in fear, we can feel powerless and vulnerable. We might try to ignore the fear, think good thoughts, pray for relief, or run and hide to gain control. Once, after trying these methods and still frozen in fear, it dawned on me: my thoughts were the cause of anxiety and distress, and I was the one choosing to listen to them. When I decided to stop listening to my fearful thoughts, I was astounded at what I heard!

This spiritual vision taught me a life-changing lesson: the energy of love can be experienced anywhere and at any time—even in moments when I am afraid. And if I want to tune in to a world of love and possibilities, it is up to me to change the channel.

EVENT

A few years ago, I visited my daughter while she was teaching at a school on a Midwest Native American reservation. One evening, a few teachers shared stories of their encounters with spirits—a common experience for those who spend time there. The tales included scary details, which made the stories interesting but left me feeling anxious. As I walked the deserted streets back to the guest house, a moving shadow caught my eye. I picked up the pace. The hairs prickled on the back of my neck—something or someone was behind me. I took a quick look over my shoulder but didn't see anything there.

When I arrived, the building was dark and empty. I was the only one staying there. I opened the creaking door and fumbled for the light switch. Taking a deep breath to settle my nerves, I began the long walk through winding hallways and up flights of stairs. Fleeting shadows disappeared around the corners. Echoes of footsteps trailed behind me. By the time I got to my room, I had sufficiently freaked myself out. I shut the door and locked it. I got into bed and settled down under the covers, convincing myself that I imagined the whole thing. Somehow, I managed to fall asleep.

About an hour later, I was startled awake by the sound of floorboards squeaking with the weight of footsteps. A door creaked open and then closed. My heart raced. I knew I was the only one staying in the guest house! I shut my eyes tightly and hoped the blindness would somehow make the noises disappear. I concentrated on my breath and prayed for relief from the fear.

I fell back to sleep yet woke again to a louder sound, and this time, it was right outside my door. I pulled the blankets over my head and covered my ears, trying to hold on to any semblance of rational thinking. With sheer determination, I forced myself to fall back asleep. After a while, the sounds woke me again, but this time, I had enough. I was tired of being afraid and exhausted by wasted efforts to console myself. I said out loud, "Come on. This is ridiculous. There is nothing to fear. Even if there are spirits here, it doesn't mean I should fear them." Having made this decision to stop listening to my fearful thoughts, I went back to sleep.

VISION

A few hours later, I am startled awake by a sound. At first, I think the spirits are back, and thoughts of danger flood my mind. I immediately feel fear. Then I remember my decision to not listen to these thoughts. I take a deep breath and relax. Much to my surprise, instead of hearing haunting noises, I hear the most beautiful sounds imaginable. It is like a symphony of drumming, chanting, and rhythmic dancing. The captivating sounds fill the night air. Soothed by the celestial music, I drift back to sleep.

An hour or so later, I awake once again to the same enchanting sounds. As I listen, I realize that it is more like a song of prayer—a hymn of love, gratitude, harmony, and communion. The energy is so powerful that it expands my awareness beyond the room, the building, and the earth to a formless state of eternal joy and peace.

As I bask in this mystical experience of expansive love, something even more amazing happens. I hear a voice speak to me! The Voice says with certainty and authority, "THIS is the true and ONLY spirit of the land. THIS and only THIS is what holds up the land. This song is an ongoing prayer that never stops. Not everyone can hear it because they are not tuned into it. And THIS is the ONLY problem."

COMMENTARY

I once heard the story of a father and son who were enjoying a day at an amusement park. After a thrilling and scary ride on the huge roller coaster, the son said to the father, "Sometimes I forget I'm the one freaking myself out." I believe this is true for most of us, and it certainly was true for me that night on the reservation.

When we are fearful, it is easy to forget that our thoughts are causing our anxiety and distress, and we are the ones choosing to listen to them. In our forgetfulness, we attempt to change the external circumstances or deny we are afraid. If that doesn't work, we "pull the covers over our head" and try to persevere.

After these futile attempts, I realized I wouldn't get much sleep if I didn't try something else. Then it occurred to me—the problem was not what was happening in the hallway. My fearful thoughts were the problem, and I could decide to stop listening to them. When I made this choice, I wasn't seeking a miracle. I was just trying to get some sleep! Imagine my surprise when this one decision led to a miraculous experience.

The next morning, I walked out of the guest house into a whole new world. What seemed frightening the night before was now alive with such powerful, loving energy that, at times, I found myself moved to tears. To this day, when I recall the memory of my experience on the reservation, my heart over-flows with love.

When I returned to my home, I noticed a profound change. As I made a conscientious effort to no longer believe every thought that crossed my mind—especially fearful thoughts, the shadows that distorted my perception disappeared. When a change occurred, I felt excitement and not anxiety. Instead of

looking at challenges as roadblocks, I perceived them as opportunities to grow and find real and lasting solutions. No longer
feeling vulnerable, I confidently shared my learnings and guided
others. Without the veil of fear, I opened my eyes to a world of
love and possibilities.

I am forever grateful for this experience and the Spirit's spoken message, which had a deep and lasting impact on me. The
words were profound yet simple. Love, not fear, is the energy
that holds all things together. This love is a part of all living
things and, therefore, exists everywhere, always. And the only
problem is that we are not "tuned in" to this energy of love. It
seems impossible to believe that THIS is the problem, especially
when we are in fear. Yet, this experience is powerful proof that
the Spirit's words are true.

Whenever you are afraid, remember the valuable lesson this
vision teaches us. We always have a choice between fear and
love. And when we decide not to listen to our fearful thoughts
and choose to "change the channel," we can experience a love
that has the power to change our world. Imagine if everyone
was tuned in to this ancient hymn of love. . . . How different
the world would be! If you were tuned in, how different would
YOUR world be?

CONTEMPLATION

To bring the heart into tune with God
is better than audible prayer.

—MARINA DE GUEVARA

+ Think of a moment or situation in your life that evokes
  fear.

✦ Become aware of the fearful thoughts racing within your mind.

✦ Recognize that you are tuned in to a station promoting danger, separation, weakness, and vulnerability.

✦ Consider that even though this is all you hear and feel right now, at the same time, there is another channel that is playing a love song. Remind yourself that tuning in to love will release fear and change the way you see your world.

✦ To tune in to love, you must first choose to stop listening to fearful thoughts. Remember, you have the power to change the channel. Do so now by stating with calm yet determined energy, "I will no longer listen to these fearful thoughts."

✦ There is nothing more you need to do. Your decision not to listen is enough. You have turned the dial to a new channel. Now, in joyful silence, listen.

✦ Be open to any feeling, sound, sense, thought, or image. Don't force it or imagine what it might be. Let it come to you naturally.

✦ Throughout the day, notice how your world appears different to you now that you are tuned in to love.

✦ If your mind slips back into fearful thoughts, remember that you can choose not to listen to them. Rest assured that you are making room for a miracle each time you choose love instead of fear.

XI.

Transforming Dis-ease through Divine Love

*Let me accept what His sight shows me as the simple truth,
and I am healed completely.*

—A COURSE IN MIRACLES

Life is full of surprises. Some unexpected events can be exciting, while others can be terrifying. When an unforeseen crisis hits, it can be easy to succumb to fear. Even after years of spiritual practice, when I heard the word "cancer," I was struck by an avalanche of fear and worry—until a sudden spiritual vision changed everything.

It may be tempting to believe that it is impossible to experience anything other than fear, pain, and upset when faced with unexpected news or devastating circumstances. If you believe this, take heart from my experience. During a moment of extreme distress, the vision I received taught me that Divine love has the power to turn any painful situation into one of peace and joy. I learned how to avoid judgment and self-criticism and instead be open to receive the gift of healing in whatever form it takes.

EVENT

In January 2004, I sit with my mom and sister awaiting the results of our mammogram screenings. We chat about our pending trip to the mall with the children and what we will cook for dinner. A nurse calls my name. The request for a second scan does not surprise me. As I walk down the hallway, last year's results, "It's only a benign cyst," echoes in my mind.

However, the next request is for an ultrasound, and that does surprise me. I remain composed until I hear the doctor order a biopsy. As I lay on the table staring at the bright lights, the doctor assures me that the additional tests do not necessarily indicate cancer. "Go about your day as planned. I'll call you with the results," she calmly instructs.

A few hours later, while standing near the merry-go-round at the mall, the phone rings. "I'm afraid I have some bad news," I hear the doctor say. I feel shaky. Careful not to alarm the kids, I walk to the nearest wall and lean in for support. "The biopsy shows aggressive cancer cells. You need to come in tomorrow to discuss our next steps."

I can think of nothing to say.

"Hello, . . . are you there?" the doctor asks.

"I'm here," I respond. But I'm not really. My mind is elsewhere. I imagine this moment without the words "cancer" and "aggressive" when instead, the doctor is saying, "Everything is fine." I then see the day ending with an enjoyable dinner with my family.

The voice of the doctor abruptly brings me back to reality. "I need to see you as soon as possible. Can you be here at 8:00 A.M. tomorrow?"

"Yes," I reply in a quivering voice.

That evening, having a few moments to myself, I think about all that I have learned as a spiritual student. I review previous times when external challenges prompted me to look internally for spiritual insights and healing. The results were always amazing. But, now I seem to be teetering between old and new habits. I can easily resort to old patterns of asking "why me?" and feeling angry and powerless. Or, I can try to apply my spiritual practice. I close my eyes and sincerely dedicate the situation to release what is untrue and to receive spiritual wisdom. I pray to the Spirit, asking for Divine wisdom and strength to guide me. I begin to relax as I settle into a warm bath.

As the tension slowly evaporates, my thoughts wander to tomorrow's appointment with the doctor. I begin to imagine what will happen to my body over the next few days and weeks ahead. Thoughts of potential pain and disfigurement threaten to dissolve my calm demeanor—a twinge of fear prickles the back of my neck. But, before it can become a wave of panic, a question pops into my mind. *All of this is happening to the body, but is it happening to me?* For one brief second, I am utterly confused about who I am. This confusion acts as a pause button. My thoughts cease, and fear dissipates. And for one glorious moment, I am completely open to whatever the answer may be.

The answer is immediate.

VISION

What happens next is difficult to describe. As best I can explain it, my perception of who I am changes dramatically. In one swift instant, my awareness "lifts" above and extends beyond my body and the room. I then become so large and expansive that now the whole universe is within me. It is as if I am looking inside a box I am holding in my hands. I see a body with cancer within the box, yet it is clear that what is happening inside the box does not affect me. With great relief, I exclaim, "Oh, I am witnessing a body with cancer, but nothing is actually happening to me!" The peace that comes with this realization is indescribable. Knowing I am safe, nothing needs to change or be different. I have never felt such freedom before.

Then I understand something of great importance. As I witness the experience of cancer unfolding, I can choose what I want to perceive and feel. Already aware of my invulnerability and feeling love, peace, and joy, what else is there to want? Without hesitation, I make my choice to experience more of the same. When I do, the curtain closes on the vision. I open my eyes. I look around. My surroundings haven't changed. But, I know this vision and choice will be life-changing.

The following morning I enter the clinic to have a second biopsy. I am in a heightened state of peace. I have no thoughts of the past, worries about the future, or judgments of any kind. And I seem to have developed x-ray vision. Permeating every person, machine, chair, and wall is the essence of God. There is so much kindness and love pouring forth from everyone; it takes great restraint not to reach out and hug them. I feel completely supported and loved. Nothing else seems to matter except this one experience of love and unity. I am ready for the next step because I know that I will experience more of the same.

When discussing surgical and chemical treatment options with the clinical staff and doctors, it is apparent that they have a sense of urgency and want to schedule surgery immediately. I remain calm. I know that no matter where I go, each person, place, or thing will continue to reveal more of God—love, beauty, and innocence. Therefore, it seems silly to judge one option as "good" or another as "bad."

I'm also aware that whatever is happening to the body will not harm me. It's as if I am wearing a Halloween costume, and I'm told, "We're going to cut your costume." Knowing that this action won't change or hurt me in any way, my response is neutral.

With these clear understandings, I peacefully agree to the doctor's treatment plan of a lumpectomy, followed by more extensive surgery.

After the lumpectomy, I go home to recuperate and await the next course of action.

While I wait, I notice a tendency to slip into fear. This trepidation mostly occurs during conversations with others about what is happening to the body. It is as if I say in response, "Oh, you're talking about me!" The minute I judge "me" as the body, I become frightened. Not because of what is happening to the body. I am afraid because I've lost sight of who I am, and I have lost sight of God's peace and love. When this occurs, I remember what it is that I genuinely want to experience. I then choose this by quietly repeating the word "God." Instantly, peace returns.

A few days later, I get the call.

There is no cancer—not even the presence of pre-cancerous cells. Nothing. The doctor is having a difficult time understanding this turn of events. She tells me that this outcome seems impossible based on the test results of the two previous biopsies. In an effort to find what was there the week before, she requested further testing of the tumor by two independent labs. "The conclusion is," she says with an incredulous tone, "not one cancer cell was found."

As I share the news with others, their reactions are understandable. One ecstatically exclaims, "You must be so thankful for the miracle!" I smile. I am thankful for the experience of unwavering peace, immense joy, and ever-present Divine love. I am grateful that I now KNOW the truth. And THIS is the real miracle.

COMMENTARY

A few months after this experience, I awoke to my clock radio alarm blaring sounds of a morning talk show. The host and a caller were discussing God and the upcoming Easter holiday. The caller shared that he was an agnostic. He wanted to believe in a loving God but did not see much evidence of one. The radio host agreed, "Yeah, when you look at such a messed-up world, it seems that God is cruel and unloving. You don't hear anyone suggesting, 'Hey, you gotta check God out!'"

I chuckled at the radio host's upside-down thinking. When we look at a world of death, sickness, poverty, and hatred, we are not seeing God. We are seeing a world that blinds us to the reality of God's peace and love.

The truth is—love is within and all around us. Regardless of what we think we see, God's love permeates and emanates from everything. There is nowhere we can go where God is absent. There is nothing we can do that would separate us from God's love. The choice to experience this love has the power to transform every moment into a miracle.

Yet, this choice doesn't seem realistic, especially when something goes wrong, and we are afraid. We believe that in order to resolve a problem, it is important to understand what it means, why it is happening and who is to blame, and then consider potential external remedies.

At one time, even Jesus's disciples thought this was important. In the biblical account of the healing of the blind man, the disciples wanted to know what caused the blindness and who was to blame. Jesus replied, "Neither hath this man sinned, nor his parents: but that the works of God should be made manifest in him" (John 9:1-3 [KJV]). We learn from Jesus's response that instead of analyzing the problem or determining cause or blame, we can choose to use every situation as an opportunity to experience the healing power of Divine love.

There is also a misunderstanding that we have to correct every false belief or have a spiritual vision of truth before being free of pain, sadness, poverty, illness, loneliness, guilt, or fear. God doesn't require us to do something before we can receive Divine gifts. We are asked only to let go of what we think the answer is and be open to receiving what the Spirit is offering. The goal is not to frighten us but to free us. The Spirit knows the perfect answer that will help us learn the truth of who we are.

You might recall the story of the man in a flood waiting for God to save him. As the water rises in the man's house, his neighbor offers him a ride. He refuses the ride stating, "God will save me." Even though the water continues to rise, he waves away a rowboat and a helicopter proclaiming, "God will save me." The man drowns. His question upon seeing God is, "I had complete devotion to You. Why didn't you save me?" God replies, "I sent you a truck, a boat, and a helicopter. What more could I do?"

This man thought he knew how God would answer his call for help. And THIS was his problem. Likewise, if we limit ourselves to what we think the answer is or how it will appear, we might say, "No, thank you," to an answer from God that would save us.

God's answer can be expressed in many ways: a remedy offered by a doctor, dinner provided by a friend, the receipt of an unexpected check in the mail, the effortless resolution of a conflict with a family member or business partner, or a vision of Divine truth. Each answer releases fear and carries the same message: you are a holy child of God and deserve His love and care.

This vision message helps us to remember that when faced with unexpected news or devastating circumstances, we can receive the gift of healing by remaining open to Divine love. Divine love is kind and gentle and seeks to serve our deepest needs and our earthly concerns. When we are open to God's abundant love, we will see it reflected in the world as health, happiness, safety, harmony, helpfulness, and peace. Then, we will be the ones saying, "Hey, you gotta check God out!"

CONTEMPLATION

To feel the love of God within you is to see the world anew, shining in innocence, alive with hope, and blessed with perfect charity and love.

—A COURSE IN MIRACLES

+ When you find yourself in a situation where healing is needed, avoid analyzing the cause or who is to blame. The past doesn't matter. It's the choice you make now— in the present moment that determines your experience.

+ Remembering that the experience of Divine love is what heals all forms of dis-ease, choose now to use this situation for this purpose.

+ Formulate in your mind what Divine love represents

to you. What would you perceive if you were aware of God's love in this situation? How would it feel?

✦ Write down whatever comes to mind, and then say it out loud.

✦ If you find yourself slipping into fear or doubt, avoid analysis and thoughts of wrongdoing or failure. These feelings merely indicate that you have lost sight of God's love. Simply restate what you want to perceive and feel until the fear and doubt dissipate.

✦ Express gratitude for your willingness to say "yes" to love—"yes" to God, and then be open to God's answer of Divine love in whatever form it appears.

XII.

Healing Guilt

This terrible mistake about yourself the miracle corrects
as gently as a loving mother sings her child to rest.

—A COURSE IN MIRACLES

The feeling of guilt is very unpleasant. It also causes us to believe that we are unworthy and unlovable. Guilt keeps us bound to the past and robs us of joy in the present. Unable to forgive ourselves, we reject love and deny our Divine nature. Therefore, if we want to awaken to our divinity and experience love, freedom, and joy, our guilt must be healed.

Are you feeling guilty because of something you did? Do you want to be free of guilt? You are not alone. But, how can we be free when our unloving actions have caused harm to others? This question plagued me for years. I felt responsible for my baby daughter's death. I wanted to be free of guilt, yet, I believed I did not deserve to be forgiven.

One morning, while reliving her death, I received a message through a vision that healed the guilt completely. I learned that guilt is not healed through punishment, apology, denial, or sacrifice. It is healed through Divine grace.

EVENT

A trip to the obstetrician confirms it—our second daughter, Amanda, will be born any day now. I have a long list of post-Christmas returns and household tasks to complete before my life becomes a stream of sleepless nights and one-minute showers. With determination and vigor, I accomplish more in one day than I thought would be possible for a woman monitoring her contractions and managing an active two-year-old. I fall asleep that night content and well-prepared for what lies ahead.

The next morning, Amanda is unusually quiet. *When did I last feel her move?* I wonder. I review the frenzied activities of the previous day, desperate to remember the moment when she said, "Hello, Mom," with an elbow jab or a kick. I pace erratically, trying to outrun the feeling of dread. *Was this moment at the grocery store, at the mall returning gifts, or talking to the bank teller? Did she move when I was changing the sheets on the beds, vacuuming, or cooking dinner?* Trembling, I reach for the phone.

Later, at the hospital, an ultrasound confirms what we feared. Teary-eyed, the doctor whispers with sadness and regret, "If only you had come in sooner." I immediately contemplate, *Does "sooner" mean yesterday? The day I was rushing around, not paying attention to her? The day I was only thinking of myself?* A groan escapes my lips. I collapse into the dark shadow of sorrow, guilt, and regret.

That night, I receive a spiritual dream that carries me through the months ahead. Eventually, I emerge from the shadows and step into a life of contentment. And sometimes, I even experience moments of happiness.

Years later, during a morning meditation, I am unexpectedly transported back to the moment in the hospital room when I heard the news. Assaulted by the inescapable sights, sounds, and feelings of the past, I do nothing to stop it. I let the tidal wave of guilt and regret wash over me.

These all-too-familiar feelings are interrupted by a startling realization: *As long as I believe I am guilty, I will not let myself experience Divine love or realize the truth of my divinity. If I am to reach my spiritual goals, I must release the guilt.* "But how is that possible?" I murmur. "Her death was my fault." Although confused, I am certain of one thing—I want to experience Divine love and know the truth of who I am. So, on this day, I do something I have not done before. I willingly hand the guilt over to the Spirit, close my eyes, and ask for healing. I surrender to whatever comes next.

VISION

I find myself back at the cemetery hovering over Amanda's tiny grave and sobbing uncontrollably. For a moment, time stands still. I feel the full weight of sorrow, guilt, and regret. Then, without warning, everything changes. I lift off the ground and soar high above the trees. Astonishingly, I no longer have a body. I am luminous and feel like I am floating. The atmosphere is bright and uplifting. I look down and see my body hovering over the grave yet, I feel free and untethered from this earthly event. Incredible love, peace, and joy envelop me.

And then I realize I am not alone. An orb of shimmering light is with me. This wise and ethereal spiritual being gently moves closer until our lights merge. Nestled in its loving, peaceful energy, I draw strength from the joining of our lights. Together we look down at the woman crying. Fully aware of my true identity, I am at peace as I witness the scene below.

A movement off to the right catches my attention. I turn and see another orb of light approaching us. I instantly recognize that this light-being is Amanda. Each movement closer to me increases the love I feel. When we touch, I feel a love so expansive that it is beyond any earthly love—even beyond the love a mother has for her child. As her light gently unites with mine, I feel spiritual emotions that cannot compare to anything I have felt on the earth plane. Words such as *joy, wonderment, unity,* and *gratitude* only capture a glimpse of the magnitude of my experience.

I know things now that were not understandable to me before. I know that we suffer because we do not realize that we are eternal spiritual beings. Believing that I was this woman, and Amanda was the baby who left me, I suffered. Now, experiencing who we are, I feel immense joy. I know that the experience of separation, although devastating at the time, has no real effect on us. It is clear that we have always been and will always be together regardless of what we experience on earth. I know that we are pure light, and the life that we share on the spiritual level is far more real than what we perceive is happening on the earth plane. I know that we can experience a profound and lasting peace when we become aware of what is real.

As I contemplate these new understandings, I hear a clear and gentle voice announce, "There is no death because she lives, and so do you. What is there to feel guilty about when there is only life and togetherness?" Upon hearing these words, the vision vanishes. I open my eyes. The guilt is gone.

I am finally free.

COMMENTARY

The stories we tell ourselves seem rooted in truth. We think we remember the events exactly as they happened. Disturbing details, especially ones that involve mistakes that caused pain, become cemented in our minds as "facts." Now, the resulting guilt and regret seem unchangeable. Retelling our stories over and over again, we give ourselves a life sentence that denies us freedom. We are not purposely trying to be unkind or unloving to ourselves. We believe we are merely reporting the "facts." And the feelings of guilt and regret that follow are unavoidable, deserved, and irrevocable.

Many religions try to help us with our stories of guilt. At the heart of these teachings is the belief that once we have harmed another through thought or deed, it is impossible to be innocent again. Therefore, the way to be free of guilt is to accept what we have done, acknowledge our guilt, and find ways to make amends. Anyone who has experienced guilt can attest to the extreme distress and limitation one feels when trying to be free in this manner. Yet, when looking at the stories from the earth plane, it seems that this is all we can do. This vision teaches us that everything changes when we are willing to perceive events from a spiritual perspective.

Willingness to change is key. Do we welcome the change from guilt to innocence? Or do we hold on to our guilt, insisting the "facts" in our story are true, and our innocence is lost forever?

It is said that Buddha once told a story of a trader who dearly loved his child. Once, while away on business, thieves raided his village and captured his five-year-old son. When the father realized his son was gone, he searched far and wide for him. He eventually discovered the unrecognizable body of a young boy. Convinced it was his son, he cremated the body, placed the ashes in a pouch, and kept it close to his heart. One day, his son escaped from the thieves and returned home. Knocking on the door late at night, the father asked, "Who is it?" The child answered, "It's me, Papa. It's your son. Open the door." Thinking that someone was playing a cruel joke on him, the father clutched the pouch and shouted, "Go away. Leave me alone." Again and again, the child knocked, but the father refused to open the door. Finally, the child walked away. The father and son never saw each other again.

We can be just like the father in this story—willing to be free of pain but refusing to let go of our version of the "truth." We cling to the "facts" so tightly that even when truth knocks on the door, we refuse to open it. I was much like the father in this story until I realized that my guilt kept me from what I desired most—love.

When I became free from this burden of guilt, I was finally able to love and trust myself again. I was willing to make mistakes and learn from them, rather than use my mistakes as proof that I was a bad person. Kinder and less critical, I was more confident in my decisions and less worried that I would make a wrong choice. As my self-confidence improved, my need for approval from others diminished. My relationships benefited, as well. I stopped trying to control others to keep them safe. I encouraged friends and family to explore opportunities outside their comfort zones and listen and follow their inner wisdom. As a result, my relationships grew into healthy bonds of honesty, freedom, and loving support. In addition, my spiritual path became much more prosperous and rewarding. After receiving this message, it was easier to let go of my "facts" and receive spiritual insights through dreams, visions, and channeled messages. Now open to loving guidance, my life naturally became more joyful.

For years I carried this story of guilt in my back pocket to remind myself that I was undeserving whenever I began to enjoy life and experience love. That is why it was important for me to acknowledge my guilt and ask for healing.

Are you holding on to an experience of guilt that limits the amount of love and joy you will allow into your life? There is no reason to be afraid to bring it out into the open. If you give it over to the Spirit of love and are open to a Divine answer, you, too, can be free.

C O N T E M P L A T I O N

So much of our memory is based upon a very subjective interpretation of events. Changing our perception through the benefit of greater understanding essentially changes the past.

—MOOJI

+ Before engaging in any healing exercise, it is important to remember that you are never alone. You are always surrounded by loving spiritual energy that can help you through all difficulties. Take a moment to acknowledge the presence of this loving energy in whatever way feels natural to you.

+ Contemplate what you desire to experience in your life. Be specific. For instance, you may want to be more confident, follow your passion, have more adventures, or deeply connect with friends and family.

+ Consider how guilt can block you from experiencing what you desire.

+ Recall the details and feelings when the guilt occurred. If you experience any resistance to remembering the event, do not force it. Instead, let your feelings arise without recalling the details. When allowing feelings to surface, it can be helpful to think of emotions like waves crashing onto the shore. They rise-up with great force, crash onto the sand, lessen in intensity, and gently float away.

✦ Express your willingness to let go of the "facts" of your story and your openness to receive spiritual insights that will heal your guilt.

✦ Refrain from thinking or imagining. Simply relax and remain open-minded.

✦ Notice any words, feelings, thoughts, images, and sensations related to your innocence. If nothing comes to mind, consider that you may need more time to let go of your "facts" in the experience. Do not judge yourself. Remind yourself that the truth is always available to you and will enter your awareness when you are ready.

✦ Give thanks for any insights you received.

✦ Throughout the days and weeks ahead, if you feel guilty, instead of responding in the old way, ask for healing. This reaction to guilt will help you remain open to receive the gift of innocence.

XIII.

Changing Darkness
into Light

If we could see ourselves and other objects as they really are,
we should see ourselves in a world of spiritual natures.

—IMMANUEL KENT

BACKGROUND

The world can appear to be a dark and scary place. Greed, selfishness, poverty, illness, ignorance, and judgment can seem to overshadow generosity, abundance, caring, health, wisdom, and support. It can be easy to conclude that these dark aspects of our world are an inevitable part of life. However, several spiritual teachings assure us that Divine light IS everywhere no matter how dark our world appears. Perceiving this ever-present light, which is the goal of many spiritual practices, will bring about miraculous changes to our world.

This perception seems impossible to believe when we experience dark and scary moments in our lives and are dominated by fear. Yet, the message received in this vision teaches that Divine light exists even in our worst nightmare. And, by making <u>one simple choice</u>, our darkened world can be transformed into a world full of light.

EVENT

As I settle into my morning routine of prayer and meditation, I feel uneasy. Recent news reports on crime, politics, and climate change, along with concerns about my children, job, and household repairs, put me in a miserable mood. The world seems dark and scary. To lift my spirits, my thoughts turn to problem-solving. I brainstorm ways to keep my children safe, enhance my career, repair the house inexpensively, save the environment, and change the political climate. After a few moments, I realize that these solutions are only temporary. There will always be problems to solve and fears to overcome. It all seems overwhelming and insurmountable. Exhausted, I stop.

There must be a spiritual solution that I have not considered, I mutter to myself. I decide to let go of my ideas and ask for spiritual insights to lead me in the right direction. I calm my breathing and close my eyes. Suddenly, my mind floods with visual imagery of my worst nightmare.

VISION

In my mind, I see myself racing down the hospital corridor. The policeman's words scream in my head: *There has been a terrible accident. Your daughter is in critical condition. Come as quickly as possible.* My heart throbs. I gasp for air. My knees buckle, yet I push myself to run.

Arriving at her room, I stop abruptly before entering. Near her door is a shimmering orb of light. Radiant and calm, yet with an air of authority, I hear, "You have a choice in how you see this. Will you choose to see this through the eyes of fear or the eyes of love?" I am stunned by this question. *A choice . . . in this situation? Impossible!* I argue silently. The firmness of the question stops me from opening the door and rushing into her room.

I consider the question.

Is it possible to see this any other way? Do I want to? If I don't experience fear, does that mean I don't care? What difference would it make if I choose love? I mull over the options: *fear or love, fear or love? Which one should I choose?* After a few seconds, without knowing what the results will be, I make my decision. "I choose love."

I push open the door and rush inside. What happens next is astonishing.

At first glance, I see a typical hospital room: bland colored walls, grayish-blue machines, an IV drip, a chair, a small window, and my daughter lying in bed perfectly still. As my mind registers these objects, I notice a bright, piercing light behind the heart monitor. I watch as a stream of light pushes through the screen and expands into the room. I then see another glimmer of light behind the IV drip pressing through the liquid bag. Simultaneously, light emerges from the chair, the ceiling, the floor, and the corners of the room. Objects disappear as rays of light pour in from everywhere. The room transitions from dark to light so quickly, I can barely take it all in.

The area around my heart feels warm. I look down to see a light radiating from my heart, feet, and hands into the room. I glance toward my daughter. Light is emanating from underneath the bed, from my daughter's heart, and the rest of her body. Soon, there is nothing in the room except pure, luminous light—and my daughter's eyes.

As I approach her, our eyes lock, and we gaze at one another. The connection is deep and intimate. Flickers of light appear behind her eyes and then expand until her eyes become pure light. In awe of this miraculous change, I am euphoric yet peaceful. I can't believe it! Heaven is here . . . in a hospital room!

In the final instant, before the vision fades, I grasp the full magnitude of the lesson: Divine light is everywhere, even in our worst nightmare. Perceiving this Divine light changes everything. It is our choice whether we see it or not.

COMMENTARY

Fear casts a shadow on our world and hides Divine light from our awareness. That is why recognizing fear is a crucial step toward enlightenment. But, acknowledging fear is not enough. We must also learn that we can choose whether to perceive darkness (fear) or light (love).

During times of distress, it can be difficult to believe that we have a choice between fear and love and that choosing love can change our dark and scary experience to one of joy. It can be challenging to accept that what we perceive in the outside world is determined by our thoughts and state of mind.

This concept reminds me of a recent television commercial for a yoga studio. In the commercial, a woman is driving her car on the expressway. Agitated, she repeatedly honks the car horn and screams at her fellow drivers. In the next scene, the same woman emerges from the yoga studio, places the yoga mat in the backseat of the car, and drives onto the expressway. Peaceful and happy, she smiles at her fellow drivers, permits cars to go ahead of her, and joyfully waves to pedestrians.

This commercial is a great reminder that if we want to live in a world of light, we must look at the world through different eyes—the eyes of love. What a surprisingly simple solution to our fear, agitation, and worry.

Gautama Buddha once told a story that reflects the same teaching:

> It easily happens that a man, when taking a bath, steps upon a wet rope, and imagines that it is a snake. Horror will overcome him and he will shake from fear, anticipating in his mind all the agonies caused by the serpent's venomous bite. What a relief does this man experience when he sees that the rope is no snake! The cause of his fright lies in his error, his ignorance, his illusion. If the true nature of the rope is recognized, his tranquility of mind will come back to him; he will feel relieved; he will be joyful and happy.

Like the man in Buddha's parable, I learned that my perceptions are not facts. And viewing life's events from a spiritual perspective (the eyes of love) can completely change how I feel, think, and act.

Moving forward, whenever I faced a troubling situation, I remembered the Spirit's guidance: "You have a choice. Will you choose to see this through the eyes of fear or through the eyes of love?" Consequently, instead of controlling the situation, making demands, denying the fear, overthinking, or running away, I considered my real choice: fear or love. Subsequently, whenever I chose love over fear, my world became brighter.

For example, during an argument with a friend, I chose to let go of my judgments and see her through the eyes of love. The unexpected awareness of her innocence and goodness quickly turned the altercation into a loving moment of connection.

Once, when I felt under attack by my neighbor during a property dispute, the choice to shift to love and compassion changed the dynamics dramatically. The situation was quickly and peacefully resolved. After the incident, we continued to remain friendly.

During a telephone conversation with another teacher, I felt unheard, unappreciated, and devalued. Feeling uncomfortable, I made excuses to end the conversation. Yet, he continued talking. Frustrated, I closed my eyes and silently declared, *I choose love.* Suddenly feeling reverence and admiration toward him, I blurted out, "I love you." We both felt the energy shift and laughed. He then confided how much he valued my opinion and appreciated all that I had taught him.

At the airport, the ticket agent warned that I could be stranded in the airport for hours, and possibly days, due to severe weather conditions. Already anxious because I was traveling alone, her harsh words only increased my anxiety. Then, I chose to feel safe and cared for regardless of the delays. By the time I approached the gate, I felt an incredible peace. The gate agent was friendly and helpful. I arrived at my destination without incident and on time.

While sitting in the marriage counselor's office, I chose to feel pure love instead of deliberately focusing on shortcomings and problems. I then had an astounding change of heart. The beauty and divinity I perceived took my breath away. As I basked in feelings of deep love and gratitude, the discussion of our issues stopped abruptly. Simultaneously, we both realized that it was time to move on. Our marriage ended peacefully and lovingly.

These are just a few examples of the marvelous shifts I experienced when I chose to see my world through the eyes of love. Sometimes I decided instantly, and other times after a few hours or days. Occasionally, I would resort to manipulation, control, or overthinking before choosing. Regardless, whenever I chose love, shifts began to happen.

If you find yourself living in a bleak and scary world where the darkness seems to have extinguished the light, remember the Spirit's question and the vision in the hospital room. No matter where you are or what is happening, Divine light IS there. And by making one simple choice, you can light up your world.

CONTEMPLATION

When you transcend the limited eyes of the ego,
you begin to see with the eyes of God.

—MOOJI

+ Take a few minutes to consider that all of life's events can be opportunities to experience contentment, harmony, joy, connection, and love.

+ Contemplate the idea that when you experience these high vibrational energies, you are making your life better and helping others release fear and feel deep, enduring love and peace.

+ Now, think of a situation (past or present) in which the dark aspects of life seem to dominate. For example, you might recall a personal crisis such as illness, loss, loneliness, financial concerns, or a global situation such as climate change, politics, poverty, or unemployment.

+ Refrain from resisting or changing the situation by reminding yourself that Divine light is beyond this shadow of fear.

+ Imagine a beautiful and radiant orb of light by your side. Feel the presence of wisdom and peace surrounding you. If you cannot sense Its presence, ask to be shown. (You can say, "I want to feel the Spirit's peace and love," or use your own words to express your desire.)

✦ Listen to the Spirit's question: "You have a choice in how you see this. Will you choose to see this through the eyes of fear or the eyes of love?"

✦ Consider the question carefully.

✦ When you are ready, make a choice. "I choose
_____."

✦ Breathe deeply and relax. Avoid the tendency to predict possible outcomes of your choice. You will only limit what is possible. Trust that the Spirit has heard your choice and is perfectly capable of bringing to you what you desire.

✦ Notice without judgment any thoughts, perceptions, emotions, and inspired actions.

✦ As each awareness comes to mind, write it down. Add to the list throughout the day.

✦ Express gratitude for each one and to yourself for your willingness to see things differently.

XIV.

Connecting to the
Spiritual Level

There is a place in you where there is perfect peace.
There is a place in you where nothing is impossible.
There is a place in you where the strength of God abides.

—A COURSE IN MIRACLES

TWO LEVELS within our mind exist simultaneously—
one ruled by the ego and the other guided by the Spirit.
When we "live" in the part of our mind where ego thoughts rule,
we experience life as scary, limiting, unsatisfying, and stressful.
As an alternative, if we move our awareness to the spiritual level
of consciousness, we experience life as safe, exciting, fulfilling,
and joyful. This makes sense when we consider the differences
between the ego level and the spiritual level of consciousness.

Thoughts on the ego level can induce fear, regret, anger,
and resentment and convince us that we are guilty and unworthy. Thoughts on the spiritual level can release us from fear,
remind us that we are loveable and deserving, and guide us to
abundance and fulfillment. Therefore, if we want a situation to
change for the better, we must connect to the spiritual level.

However, crossing the threshold from one level of consciousness to another can be challenging.

When a man asked Jesus what he needed to do to enter the kingdom of heaven, Jesus replied that it is easier for a camel to pass through the eye of a needle than it is for a rich man to enter the kingdom of God (Matthew 19:24 [KJV]). In other words, the threshold between the ego level and the spiritual level is narrow. If we cling to ego thoughts, desires, and solutions, we cannot fit through the narrow frame. Yet, for many of us, letting go is not easy.

The following story illustrates how difficult it is for us to let go of ego thoughts, even though holding on to them is unsatisfying and painful.

A woman approached a spiritual guru asking for help. "I am sad and lonely," she began. "I have been betrayed by my friends, criticized by my parents, and ignored by my children. Please help me."

With infinite patience and compassion, the guru replied, "If you want to feel love, joy, and peace, you must let go of these thoughts."

"What?" the woman exclaimed. "But you don't understand. Everyone hates me. You wouldn't believe how others treat me."

With infinite patience and compassion, he replied, "Let go of these thoughts as well."

The woman began to cry. "You don't get it," she whispered through her tears. "I was abandoned and left all alone."

With infinite patience and compassion, the guru replied, "Let go of these thoughts as well."

The woman became angry. "I can't!" she argued. "They're true. I can't let them go."

With infinite patience and compassion, the guru remained silent.

At times I was like the woman in this story. One evening, while drowning in a pool of ego thoughts and emotions, I prayed for relief. The Spirit offered me the same advice as the guru. An image appeared in my mind of my hands clutching a cactus plant with long, prickly needles. I then heard a gentle voice say, "Just let go." Even though I understood the message and wanted relief from the pain, I felt powerless to stop listening to them. I cried out, "How can I let them go?"

I received the answer in a dream.

DREAM

In the dimly lit house that I share with friends, life is monotonous. Today my housemates are playing a card game to occupy their time. Uninterested, I look around for something to do. "I suppose I could watch TV," I sigh. These dull living conditions are getting difficult to bear. To make matters worse, we share our living space with an uninvited, annoying roommate (the ego). Appearing as a little man, he acts childish and wants to be the center of attention. He needs constant entertainment. He is never satisfied and overly critical. Right on cue, he tugs on my sleeve and whines, "What should I play with next? I'm bored." Deflated, I slump in my chair. I'm not sure how much longer I can tolerate living like this.

I glance to my right and notice a hallway off the living room. "Is that new?" I wonder. Wait . . . I remember now. This hallway leads to another part of the house! I survey our current living conditions: A friend vacuums the living room rug, a few others play board games, while our little roommate annoys everyone with his constant chatter. "Whatever is on the other side of the house must be better than living like this," I mutter to myself. I am determined to leave.

I gather my friends together. Careful not to alert our roommate, we squeeze into a huddle and speak in hushed tones. "We can leave!" I announce in a loud whisper.

"Leave? But where would we go?" asks a friend.

"There is a hallway that leads to another part of the house," I explain. "I don't know what it's like to live there, but I'm going anyway. Are you with me?"

After a momentary pause, they reply in unison, "Yes!"

"Shhh," I plead, pointing to the little man who is coloring at the kitchen table. "We can't take him with us. We need to distract him so he doesn't follow us. I have an idea."

We engage in a few more conspiratorial whispers, and then we take action.

We entice our roommate to go into the bedroom with the promise of many toys. Enthralled by the shiny trinkets, noisy trucks, and stuffed animals, he doesn't notice the door closing. We tiptoe toward the hallway. I take the lead. Everyone follows in single file down the long, narrow hallway. "This is very exciting," a voice behind me says softly. "I can't wait to see what is on the other side of the house."

Arriving at the end of the hallway, I hold the door open and gesture for my friends to cross the threshold. Suddenly, a piercing screech stops everyone in their tracks. "Don't leave me. I can't survive without you!" We turn around to see the little man running toward us. He looks forlorn and terrified.

I know that his heartfelt pleas are a trick to keep us from leaving, but the others do not. A few friends take steps toward him. "Do not listen to him," I state firmly. "He is trying to trick you into staying. Ignore everything he says and keep walking."

The friends in the front of the line reluctantly follow my instructions and cross the threshold. This action causes another heart-wrenching plea from the little man. "Please, please don't leave me."

"Shouldn't we help him?" a friend asks. The others nod in agreement, their resolve weakening. I remain resolute.

Recognizing that his cries are a ploy to get us to stay, I command, "Do not listen to him. Keep walking!" My certainty keeps everyone moving forward . . . except the girl at the end of the line. I sense that she feels guilty for leaving him behind. His clever tactic is working.

She looks at me, glances at the little man, and then stares back at me. "He needs me," she counters, "I should pick him up."

She runs to the little man, swings him up onto her back, and walks toward me.

I cross the threshold, turn around, and make one last attempt to persuade her. "Please put him down," I plead. "You can't bring him with you. If you hold onto him, you won't be able to cross the threshold and live in the other part of the house." Even though she realizes this is true, she cannot bring herself to let him go. Sadly, I watch as the door closes.

I turn around and become aware of my new surroundings. The furniture, floors, and walls are sparkling white. People dressed in soft shimmering robes float effortlessly around the room. Exhilarated by sounds of laughter and lively conversations, my skin tingles with excitement. I feel alive!

A woman with kind eyes floats toward me. She beckons me to follow her into another room. I stand at the doorway. My daughter is lying on a bed, holding her newborn baby. I race to her side. Tenderly, she kisses the baby's forehead and says, "Her name is Cherished, which means blessings."

This beautiful new life fills my heart with joy. I can't believe that when we were living in the dull and lifeless part of the house, there existed these beautiful, light-filled rooms! If I hadn't decided to leave, we would have missed all this beauty. My heart bursts with gratitude that I remembered this part of the house and that we made the choice to live here.

This dream message is a reminder that the ego is not a powerful wizard who can control what we think or what we do, nor does the ego have our best interest at heart. The ego is a frightened little voice within our mind that has only one objective: self-preservation. It will say whatever is necessary to keep our attention and prevent us from connecting to the spiritual level. When this happens, we may be unable or unwilling to "walk away" from the ego.

There are various reasons why we choose to "live" with the ego. We may cling to painful and fearful thoughts believing that we are powerless to let them go. We may feel uncomfortable leaving familiar solutions behind. We may be convinced that we need the ego to protect us from harm or satisfy our deepest desires. These doubts and fears are the ego trying to prevent us from connecting to the spiritual level.

The ego knows our vulnerabilities and uses them to keep us engaged. If you are tempted to listen to the ego's threats and empty promises, do not judge yourself. Instead, with infinite patience and compassion, pause and consider your choices. You can hold on to ego thoughts and remain on the ego level of consciousness, or you can drop the ego and step across the threshold into a "world" of light and love.

✦ ✦ ✦

The dreams and visions in this book are examples of what can happen when you take a chance and decide to leave the ego level in pursuit of spiritual answers. When you connect to the spiritual level and, as a result, experience safety, joy, love, and inspiration, you will be happy that you remembered this part of your mind and that you chose to "live" there.

XV.

Dreaming Miracles is
Everyone's Gift

*God gives no special favors, and no one has any powers
that are not available to everyone.*

—A Course in Miracles

S PIRITUAL DREAMS are an amazing resource we
can use to live life miraculously. When we allow God
to speak to us in dreams, we become open to profound changes
that affect ourselves, those closest to us, and the world around
us. Because of this, nothing would make me happier than to
know that this book helped you to "enter the secret passageway"
and receive your spiritual messages.

Everyone dreams. Even if you don't think you dream, science
has proven that you do. And, even though you might not have
accessed spiritual wisdom in your dreams, it is there. My first
dream came with no forewarning. It occurred during the darkest
hours of my life. It was an unexpected and unsought answer to
the deepest pain of human existence—the pain of separation.
This experience helped me realize that anyone, at any time, no
matter how much pain or fear they are in, can receive support,
guidance, and healing through their dreams.

However, to use this gift consistently and more effectively, I learned the importance of developing a strong foundation in our waking life. We must first practice self-awareness. This practice includes being honest and open about our feelings, beliefs, and fears. The more we are willing to explore the contents of the "basement" (our unconscious), the better our chances of discovering the "secret passageway" that leads to spiritual wisdom.

Another essential building block to spiritual dreaming is cultivating a love for ourselves, others, and God. By making a conscious effort to let go of judgment and focus on love, we connect with a deeper spiritual perspective.

Equally important to a strong foundation is using the nightly dream practice included in this book. This practice opens our heart and mind to receive spiritual messages and increases our willingness and determination to reach far beyond the ego's limited ideas. In essence, this practice puts our mind into a receptive state and becomes the bridge that connects us from one level of consciousness to another.

Finally, how we interpret the message is key. If we discern a spiritual message through the lens of the ego, we dilute its healing power and its ability to teach us the truth. Therefore, allowing the interpretation of the dream to be guided by the Spirit is of utmost importance. This step involves letting go of what we think we know, becoming still, and asking for insights and direction.

When combining a nightly practice with a strong foundation, spiritual dreams become more consistent, effective, and miraculous.

God is speaking to you from deep within your mind. Why not begin listening tonight?

XVI.

A Guide to Dreaming Miracles

*Dreams are for the purpose of directing us to higher and more
balanced accomplishments in our physical,
mental and spiritual lives.
Dreams work to solve the problems of the dreamer's
conscious waking life
and to quicken in the dreamer new potentials which are
his or hers to claim.*

—EDGAR CAYCE

BEFORE YOU BEGIN

1. Obtain a notebook specifically for supporting your dream practice.

2. In your notebook, list the reasons you want to receive spiritual dream messages. (I wish to obtain guidance, restore harmony to my relationships, receive answers to my questions, or become aware of unconscious beliefs and behavior patterns.)

3. Formalize a written commitment to your dream practice and include the following:

   a. I will devote (*x* days, *x* weeks, *x* months) to using my nighttime dreams as a channel to receive messages from the spiritual realm.

b. I will document my dream upon waking. (If not, I might not recall important details.)

c. I will set aside (choose a time each day) to study my dreams and reflect on their messages.

d. I will make a daily effort to apply the messages I receive.

e. When inspired, I will share my dreams so they can be used to help others.

f. I will give thanks for every dream message I receive, even if it makes me feel uncomfortable. I understand that as I take steps to seek answers and guidance, learn, and grow, I may experience discomfort.

DREAMING MIRACLES NIGHTTIME PRACTICE

STEP ONE: DETERMINE REQUEST

1. As you settle into bed, think about an issue, decision, challenge, or event you would like insight into and write it down.

2. Write down any feelings and thoughts that arise when you consider the situation.

3. Use this information to formulate a concise question that you would like an answer to and write it down. The question can be as specific as "What house should I buy?" or as general as "What do I need to be aware of right now?"

4. Say the question out loud or silently to yourself.

STEP TWO: RELAX

Your willingness to receive spiritual insight and the Spirit's desire and power to communicate with you are energies needed to receive a spiritual message.

Trust that these energies are already in place and then breathe deeply and slowly relax into a peaceful state of mind.

STEP THREE: INVITE THE ANSWER, LET GO OF THE OUTCOME

1. Create and say a prayer that includes elements of trust, willingness, and gratitude or, recite one of the following:

   + *I pray and trust that Divine wisdom will gently offer guidance while I sleep. I ask that my dreams be used as a source of healing for myself and others. I accept whatever message and form of communication is best for me at this time. When I awaken, I will remember the dream. Thank you for answering the prayers of my heart.*

   + *All-knowing, Universal Source, please communicate with me through my dreams tonight. I am open to any insight and guidance that is most helpful and beneficial to me and others. When I awaken, I will remember the dream. Thank you for your Divine love and guidance.*

STEP FOUR: RECALL

1. When you wake up, do not get out of bed! Quietly, ask yourself, "Did I have a dream last night?" Then let your mind naturally recall any nighttime image, activity, event, person, place, or feeling.

2. In your notebook, document all the dream details even if you perceive some details as insignificant. Describe how you feel now after experiencing the dream.

3. Express gratitude for the dream; *THEN* get out of bed.

4. As you go about your day, note any additional details of the dream that you recall.

STEP FIVE: STUDY

1. Review your dream notes. Then, close your eyes and mentally recreate the dream.

2. As you recall the situation, characters, images, and emotions from the dream, ask yourself:

   + *How do I feel?*

   + *What do the images and the setting mean to me?*

   + *How does this dream provide an understanding of my problem, block, or pattern?*

   + *What unconscious beliefs and emotions were revealed?*

3. Seek further insights and guidance by meditating on the following: *How does this dream answer my question or fulfill my intention?* Be still and listen for answers. Note anything that comes to mind.

4. Document and express gratitude for the key insights and guidance received.

STEP SIX: APPLY

1. Contemplate how you can apply the insights and guidance to your current situations and relationships.

2. Follow through with a commitment to apply what you have learned.

XVII.

My Grateful Heart

You do not walk alone.
God's angels hover near and all about.
His Love surrounds you, and of this be sure;
that I will never leave you comfortless.

—A COURSE IN MIRACLES

O N T H E first anniversary of Amanda's death, I was grief-stricken and had fallen back into a deep, dark place. I wondered if I would ever laugh again, enjoy the pleasantries of life, or happily engage with the people I loved. I had read that cultivating an attitude of gratitude was a way to shift from despair to happiness. I balked at this concept. Taking care of my daughter and completing normal household tasks were overwhelming. How could I feel grateful when I could barely get out of bed or stop crying? I went to bed that night, believing that my pain and sorrow would never end. I struggled to feel grateful for anything. Weary and dispirited, I fell asleep, crying a simple prayer, "Please, God. Help me."

During the night, I had my second spiritual dream, which taught me that there is indeed a reason to feel grateful. We learn from this dream that it is easy to have a grateful heart when given a vision of the future and its' many blessings.

DREAM

I stand in a darkened hallway, confused and alone. Without direction or a goal, life seems pointless. Peering through the darkness, I notice a closed door at the far end of the hallway. The solid wall behind me determines my direction. I take a step forward; it is my only choice.

The walls on both sides guide me along the path. "At least I can't lose my way." Comforted by this thought, I continue walking. I arrive at the door, indifferent to what is on the other side. What else is there to do but open it? Tightening my grip on the knob, I turn it, push the door forward, and step over the threshold. The view takes my breath away—golden rays of light cascade over the spacious room's walls, pillars, and marble floor. My eyes glance upward, tracing the source of light. Streaming through a large opening in the gilded dome ceiling is a brilliant golden ball of light. It seems to originate from the heavens above. As I look around, I am in awe of my new surroundings. And—I am not alone.

More than one hundred people hold hands in a circle in the middle of the room, poised to recite a prayer. They pause before they begin, and I somehow know that they are waiting for me to join them. Two people unlock their hands and welcome me. Reverently, I step forward, take their hands, and close the gap. The circle is complete.

Glancing around the circle, I wonder, "Who will be the one to lead us in prayer?" Surprisingly, they look at me. "Am I the one to lead? I have no idea what to say." I dismiss these doubtful thoughts with an inner knowing; my path had always been leading me to this exact moment. Trusting that this inner knowing would guide me, I open my mouth to speak. It is not words that come forth, but a sound—a beautiful single note that reverberates throughout the room. I feel charged with its electrifying energy. Love and peace are palpable. The sweet, joyful vibration is contagious. I watch as each person feels this wave of energy and spontaneously adds their voice to the celestial note—until the grand room fills with the sound of angels.

Upon waking, my attitude about gratitude had completely shifted. I immediately took pen to paper and made a gratitude list. My entries included: gratitude for my inner wisdom, the spiritual messages I received, the Creator's limitless love for me, Divine comfort and guidance, and what was yet to come into my life.

At the time, I did not know that I would receive more spiritual messages or become an author. I did not know the people in the circle who would help me share these messages with the world. Today, I know them by name.

I am eternally grateful to the many people who helped me reach the doorway, enter the celestial room, and experience joy.

Writing a book is not for the faint of heart. When students attending my classes urged me to write a book of spiritual messages, I hesitated. Capturing the beauty and profound teachings of my dreams and visions was a daunting task. More so, it would require me to share intimate details of my experiences, which I preferred to keep private. The ego's loud, "No way!" response was eventually drowned out by the students' enthusiasm and unrelenting pleas to have these messages in writing. I owe a debt of gratitude to those who would not take "no" for an answer. Without them, *Dreaming Miracles* would have remained sequestered in my dream journal.

Words cannot express how grateful I am for the love and support from my friends and family. When I announced that I would take time off from teaching to write a book, they replied without hesitation, "Go for it!" Their faith in me was an amazing gift. More than that, they cheered me on in several ways: proofreading my writing, researching references, providing encouraging words, offering financial help, and freeing me from hours of solitude with a meal, a walk, or a game of pickleball. I am blessed to have so many caring and supportive people in my life.

The assistance of a gifted editor is essential to any writing project. When God provides a talented editor in the form of a friend, one is doubly blessed. Cheryl Leisner's commitment to this book was extraordinary. She exemplified tremendous patience and expertise during endless hours of revision and discussion. Her acute sixth sense about the best way to express the Spirit's messages ensured the teachings' accuracy. I am deeply grateful for her vision and faith in the transformational power of the messages I received. Her devotion to this project has earned her angel wings.

With deep admiration, I thank my mentors, who gently demanded that I grow and stretch way beyond my comfort level. They urged me to ask questions and keep asking until the answers felt right. They taught me to embrace every moment as an opportunity to grow, no matter how challenging the situation. Their teachings guided and inspired me to connect to my inner Spirit and honor the messages I received. Leading by example, these guardian angels remain a beacon of light for us all.

A sincere and heartfelt thank you to the publishing team at Sunbury Press. A special thanks to Lawrence Knorr for taking a chance on a first-time author, recognizing the value of the dream and vision messages, and committing to completing the project. Thank you to Abigail Henson for her keen insight and editorial skill. She entered my life at a time when I needed fresh ideas and a burst of enthusiasm. Her contributions were invaluable to this project.

Lastly, I honor my Spirit, my trusted Friend, my True Self, who hears my call and answers with love, wisdom, humor, and miracles.

References

Abraham-Hicks Facebook Page, accessed August 27, 2019, www.facebook.com/pg/Abraham.Hicks/posts/. December 22, 2014. www.Abrahamhicks.com.

A Course in Miracles Combined Volume. 2nd ed., 1975. Tiburon, CA: Foundation for Inner Peace, 1992.

A Course in Miracles: Complete & Annotated Edition. Edited by Robert Perry. West Sedona, AZ: Circle of Atonement, 2017.

"A Course in Miracles Study Group with Raj." *The Raj Materials*. Northwest Foundation for A Course in Miracles. www.nwffacim.wordpress.com/2016/08/03/acim-study-group-august-2nd/. 2016, August 2.

Blatz, Beate. *The Coptic Gospel of Thomas. New Testament Apocrypha*. Vol. 1. Rev. ed. Edited by Wilhelm Schneemelcher. 113. Translated by R. McL. Wilson, Louisville: Westminster John Knox, 1991.

Carus, Paul. *The Gospel of Buddha According to Old Records*. London, England: Open Court Publishing Company, 1895.

Cayce, Edgar. *Dreams & Visions*. Virginia Beach, VA: A.R.E. Press, 2008.

Collier, Robert. *The Secret of the Ages*. New York, NY: Robert Collier Publications, 1926. www.robertcollierpublications.com.

De Guevara, Marina. *Letters*. 16th Century. *The Quotable Spirit*. Compiled and Edited by Peter Lorie and Manuela Dunn Mascetti. Edison, NJ: Castle Books, 1996.

Jung, Carl Gustav. *The Practice of Psychotherapy*. Translated by R.F.C. Hull. Princeton, NJ: Princeton University Press, 1966.

Kant, Immanuel. *Critique of Pure Reason*. 1781. Translated by J.M.D. Meiklejohn. London, England: George Bell and Sons, 1901.

King, Hans Christian. *Stop Searching and Start Living: Manifest the Life You Were Born to Live*. Wheeling, IL: Nightingale-Conant Corp, May 2004.

Rogers, Carl R. *On Becoming a Person: A Therapist's View of Psychotherapy*. New York, NY: Houghton Mifflin, 1961.

Thich, Nhat Hanh. *Finding our True Home: Living in the Pure Land Here and Now*. Berkeley, CA: Parallax Press, 2004.

About the Author

PATTI FIELDS – an intuitive dreamer and interpreter and a well-respected teacher of *A Course in Miracles* (ACIM) and spiritual dream work, experienced her first spiritual dream in the darkest moment of her life. With the sudden opening of this communication channel, Patti began to receive transformational messages for herself and others. She shares these messages in her books, programs, articles, and recordings to support and encourage others to connect to Divine wisdom for help and healing. Patti's honesty, warmth, humor, and practical application of these spiritual teachings guide others to experience miracles—complete freedom from years of old beliefs, patterns, trauma, and pain. Patti lives in Rochester, NY and enjoys connecting with family and friends, and playing pickleball—where she finds many opportunities to apply her spiritual practice on the court.

✦

Additional resources pertaining to *Dreaming Miracles* and *A Course in Miracles* (articles, audio recordings, videos, and service offerings) are available at:

www.pattifields.com,

Facebook@AwakeningThroughDreamsandVisions, and

www.youtube.com/c/PattiFieldsMiracles

Made in the USA
Middletown, DE
23 June 2021

42167255R00071